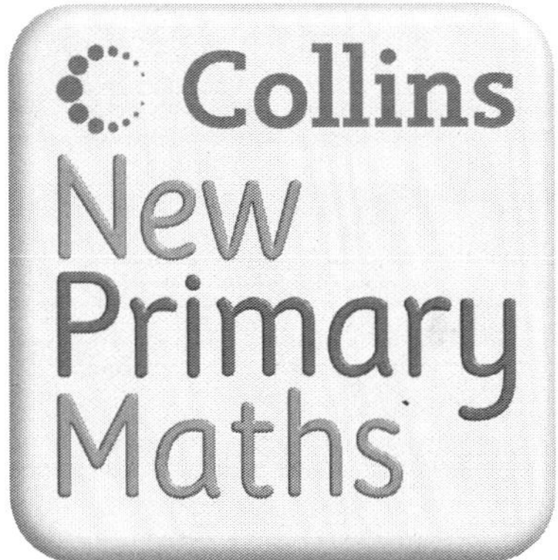

Speaking and Listening Foundation

Developing children's listening skills
in the daily maths lesson

Peter Clarke

William Collins' dream of knowledge for all began with the publication of his first book in 1819. A self-educated mill worker, he not only enriched millions of lives, but also founded a flourishing publishing house. Today, staying true to this spirit, Collins books are packed with inspiration, innovation and practical expertise. They place you at the centre of a world of possibility and give you exactly what you need to explore it.

Collins. Freedom to teach.

Published by Collins
An imprint of HarperCollins*Publishers* Ltd.
77-85 Fulham Palace Road
Hammersmith
London
W6 8JB

Browse the complete Collins catalogue at www.collinseducation.com

© HarperCollins*Publishers* Ltd 2009

10 9 8 7 6 5 4 3

ISBN: 978-0-00-732278-7

Peter Clarke asserts his moral right to be identified as the author of this work.

Any educational institution that has purchased one copy of this publication may make unlimited duplicate copies for use exclusively within that institution. Permission does not extend to reproduction, storage within a retrieval system, or transmittal in any form or by any means, electronic, mechanical, photocopying, recording or otherwise, of duplicate copies for loaning, renting or selling to any other institution without the permission of the Publisher.

British Library Cataloguing in Publication Data
A Catalogue record for this publication is available from the British Library.

Cover template: Laing&Carroll
Cover illustration: Jonatronix Ltd.
Series design: Neil Adams
Illustrations: Bethan Matthews, Jeffrey Reid, Lisa Williams, Mel Sharp, Rhiannon Powell

Acknowledgement
The author wishes to thank Brian Molyneaux for his valuable contribution to this publication.

Printed and bound by Martins the Printers Ltd

FSC is a non-profit international organisation established to promote the responsible management of the world's forests. Products carrying the FSC label are independently certified to assure consumers that they come from forests that are managed to meet the social, economic and ecological needs of present and future generations.

Find out more about HarperCollins and the environment at
www.harpercollins.co.uk/green

Contents

Introduction

Collins New Primary Maths: Speaking and Listening is a series of seven books from Foundation to Year 6 which is designed to assist children in practising and consolidating objectives from the *Renewed Primary Framework for Mathematics* (2006) at the same time as developing their listening skills.

Listening and following instructions are two key skills that are crucial to the success of every child and every adult. How many times have children had to redo work because they have not listened to your directions? How many times do you have to repeat yourself? How often have you wished you could take time out from the overburdened curriculum to help children develop their listening skills? This series will help you solve these problems. You will not have to take time away from other curriculum areas to do this since *Collins New Primary Maths: Speaking and Listening* helps to develop children's listening skills and ability to follow oral directions while they practise valuable mathematical skills.

Listening and communicating

The purpose of this book is the development of children's listening skills through the mathematics curriculum, but this skill is not seen in isolation. Many of the activities outlined include reading, speaking and writing. Listening is an integral part of communication which deals with the process of giving and receiving information. The four different aspects of the communication process outlined below rely upon each other for effective communication at the same time as actively supporting and enriching one another.

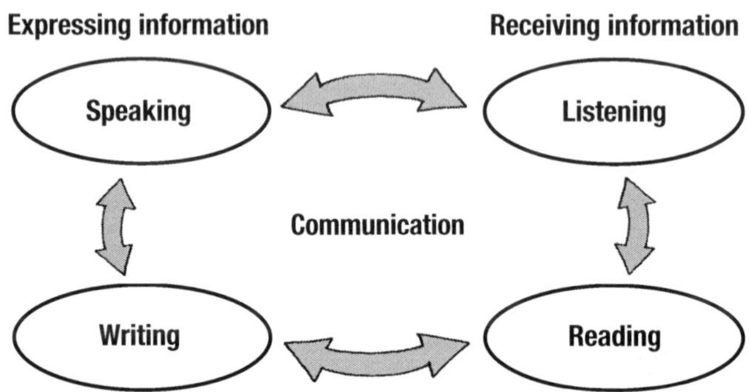

Communication and mental imagery

All children, whatever their age and ability, have their own mental images, developed from previous knowledge and experiences. Aural stimulus enables children to manipulate the mental images they have of numbers, shapes and measures. Instant recall of number facts such as the multiplication tables and the addition and subtraction number facts often depends on an aural input. Children have to hear the sounds in order to give an automatic response.

The difficult part for the teacher is to discover what is going on inside children's heads. This is where discussion as an accompaniment to mental work is so important. It is only through discussion that the teacher can begin to develop an insight into children's mental processes. Discussions also enable children to develop their own insights into their mental imagery and provide the opportunity for them to share their ideas and methods. They can form judgements about the alternatives, decide which methods are the most efficient and effective for them, and further develop flexibility and familiarity with the different mathematical topics.

The skills of listening

Listening skills can be improved through training and practice. When direct attention is paid to listening for specific purposes, and these skills are practised and consolidated, improvement in ability follows. In general children tend to learn and remember more through listening than in almost any other way. A high percentage of all the information children receive comes through their ears. Thus direct training in the skills of listening can be hugely beneficial to all learning.

Effective listening involves:

- hearing
- concentrating
- a knowledge of language
- a knowledge of the structure of language
- recognising cues
- being able to contextualise
- inferring
- thinking
- processing
- summarising
- selecting
- organising
- drawing upon previous knowledge and experience
- comprehending/understanding the main idea.

Becoming a good listener

Display the poster on page 6 to remind children of how to become a good listener. When concentrating on developing children's listening skills draw attention to the poster.

Characteristics of a good listener

A good listener is one who:

- knows how to listen
- is able to concentrate on listening
- looks at the speaker
- is courteous to the speaker
- does not interrupt the speaker
- is able to zero in on the speaker and eliminate extraneous noises and interruptions
- can comprehend
- is selective
- asks him/herself questions while listening
- draws upon their previous knowledge and experiences
- evaluates while listening
- remembers what is said
- anticipates what is coming next.

Good listening

Sit still

Think about the words

Look at the speaker

Collins New Primary Maths: Speaking and Listening Foundation © HarperCollins*Publishers* Ltd 2009

Collins New Primary Maths: Speaking and Listening and the teaching–learning cycle

Assessment

- Each activity can be used to assess a specific objective from the *Renewed Primary Framework for Mathematics* (2006).
- Guidance given on how to record pupil performance.

Planning

- Each activity linked to an objective in the *Renewed Primary Framework for Mathematics* (2006)
- Guidance given for planning a programme of work.

Teaching

- Clear and complete instructions given for each activity.
- Ideally suited to the daily mathematics lesson.

Curriculum information

Each of the 30 activities is organised under specific objectives as identified in the *Renewed Primary Framework for Mathematics* (2006). The *Collins New Primary Maths: Speaking and Listening* objectives coverage chart on page 8 shows which activity is matched to which objective(s).

Planning a programme of work for *Collins New Primary Maths: Speaking and Listening*

The *Collins New Primary Maths: Speaking and Listening* programme chart on page 9 may be used in conjunction with your long- and medium-term plans to develop a *Collins New Primary Maths: Speaking and Listening* programme of work throughout the year. By following the Blocks and Units from the *Renewed Primary Framework for Mathematics* (2006) you will ensure that the children have the opportunity to practise and consolidate the strands, and specific objectives for a particular unit of work, at the same time as developing their listening skills.

Collins New Primary Maths: Speaking and Listening and the daily mathematics lesson

The activities contained in *Collins New Primary Maths: Speaking and Listening* are ideally suited to the daily mathematics lesson. Each activity is designed to be presented to the whole class. The activities are extremely flexible and can be used in a variety of ways. For example, activities can be used during the:

- oral work and mental calculation session to practise and consolidate previously taught concepts;
- main teaching part of the lesson to focus on particular skills and concepts;
- plenary session to consolidate the concept(s) taught during the main part of the lesson and to conclude the lesson in an enjoyable way.

***Collins New Primary Maths: Speaking and Listening* objectives coverage**

STRAND	OBJECTIVES	ACTIVITY	PAGE
1: Using and applying mathematics	**Talk about, recognise and recreate simple patterns**	1	12
	Sort objects, making choices and justifying decisions	2	14
	Use developing mathematical ideas and methods to solve practical problems	3	16
	Use developing mathematical ideas and methods to solve practical problems (in the context of money)	4	18
2: Counting and understanding number	**Say and use the number names in order in familiar contexts**	5	20
	Count aloud in ones	6	22
	Count reliably up to 10 everyday objects	7	24
	Recognise numerals 1 to 9	8	26
	Recognise (and record) **numerals 1 to 9**	9	28
	Use language such as 'more' or 'less' to compare two numbers	10	30
	Compare two numbers (and say a number that lies between them)	11	32
	Use the number names in order Order a set of numbers	12	34
	Use ordinal numbers in different contexts	13	36
3: Knowing and using number facts	Select two groups of objects to make a given total of objects	14	38
	Find one more or one less than a number from 1 to 10	15	40
4: Calculating	**In practical activities and discussion begin to use the vocabulary involved in adding Begin to relate addition to combining two groups of objects**	16	42
	In practical activities and discussion begin to use the vocabulary involved in subtracting Begin to relate subtraction to 'taking away'	17	44
	In practical activities and discussion begin to use the vocabulary involved in adding and subtracting (Separate (partition) a given number of objects into two groups)	18	46
	In practical activities and discussion begin to use the vocabulary involved in adding and subtracting Begin to find out how many have been removed from a larger group of objects by counting up from a number.	19	48
	In practical activities and discussion begin to use the vocabulary involved in adding and subtracting Work out by counting how many more are needed to make a larger number.	20	50
5: Understanding shape	**Use language such as 'circle' or 'bigger' to describe the shape and size of flat shapes**	21	52
	Use language such as 'bigger' to describe the shape and size of solids shapes	22	54
	Use familiar objects and common shapes to create and recreate patterns	23	56
	Use everyday words to describe position	24	58
6: Measuring	**Use language such as 'greater' or 'smaller' to compare quantities** (length)	25	60
	Use language such as 'greater', 'smaller', 'heavier' or 'lighter' to compare quantities (mass)	26	62
	Use language such as 'greater' or 'smaller' to compare quantities (capacity)	27	64
	Use everyday language related to time; order and sequence familiar events	28	66
	Use everyday language related to time; order and sequence familiar events (Begin to know the days of the week in order)	29	68
	Use everyday language related to time (Begin to read o'clock time)	30	70

All statements and wording in bold refer to the Early Learning Goals.

Collins New Primary Maths: Speaking and Listening programme

YEAR
CLASS
TEACHER

	UNIT	MATHEMATICS STRANDS	*CNPM: SPEAKING AND LISTENING* ACTIVITY
AUTUMN	A1	**Counting, partitioning and calculating** Strand 1: Using and applying mathematics Strand 2: Counting and understanding number Strand 3: Knowing and using number facts Strand 4: Calculating	
	B1	**Securing number facts, understanding shapes** Strand 1: Using and applying mathematics Strand 3: Knowing and using number facts Strand 5: Understanding shape	
	C1	**Handling data and measures** Strand 1: Using and applying mathematics Strand 6: Measuring Strand 7: Handling data	
	D1	**Calculating, measuring and understanding shape** Strand 1: Using and applying mathematics Strand 4: Calculating Strand 5: Understanding shape Strand 6: Measuring	
	E1	**Securing number facts, calculating, identifying relationships** Strand 1: Using and applying mathematics Strand 2: Counting and understanding number Strand 3: Knowing and using number facts Strand 4: Calculating	
SPRING	A2	**Counting, partitioning and calculating** Strand 1: Using and applying mathematics Strand 2: Counting and understanding number Strand 3: Knowing and using number facts Strand 4: Calculating	
	B2	**Securing number facts, understanding shapes** Strand 1: Using and applying mathematics Strand 3: Knowing and using number facts Strand 5: Understanding shape	
	C2	**Handling data and measures** Strand 1: Using and applying mathematics Strand 6: Measuring Strand 7: Handling data	
	D2	**Calculating, measuring and understanding shape** Strand 1: Using and applying mathematics Strand 4: Calculating Strand 5: Understanding shape Strand 6: Measuring	
	E2	**Securing number facts, calculating, identifying relationships** Strand 1: Using and applying mathematics Strand 2: Counting and understanding number Strand 3: Knowing and using number facts Strand 4: Calculating	
SUMMER	A3	**Counting, partitioning and calculating** Strand 1: Using and applying mathematics Strand 2: Counting and understanding number Strand 3: Knowing and using number facts Strand 4: Calculating	
	B3	**Securing number facts, understanding shapes** Strand 1: Using and applying mathematics Strand 3: Knowing and using number facts Strand 5: Understanding shape	
	C3	**Handling data and measures** Strand 1: Using and applying mathematics Strand 6: Measuring Strand 7: Handling data	
	D3	**Calculating, measuring and understanding shape** Strand 1: Using and applying mathematics Strand 4: Calculating Strand 5: Understanding shape Strand 6: Measuring	
	E3	**Securing number facts, calculating, identifying relationships** Strand 1: Using and applying mathematics Strand 2: Counting and understanding number Strand 3: Knowing and using number facts Strand 4: Calculating	

How to use *Collins New Primary Maths: Speaking and Listening*

Preparation

- Provide each child with the necessary resources. These can be found at the beginning of each activity's teacher's page.

Instructions

Explain the following to the children:

- They need to listen carefully.
- They will be given some oral instructions to follow.
- The instructions will only be given once.
- They must only do what they are told to do, nothing more.
- They may not use an eraser.
- How many instructions there are for the particular activity.
- That they are to do each task immediately after the instructions for that part have been given.

The activity

- If necessary, briefly discuss the pupil sheet with the children. Ensure that the children are familiar with the pictures and/or the text on the sheet.
- Ensure that the children are also familiar with any of the terms used in the oral instructions. Refer to the *Key words* for a list of the relevant vocabulary.
- Ask the children to write the date on the sheet in the space provided.
- Do not ask the children to write their name. This will occur during the activity.
- Slowly read the instructions to the children.

Discussion

- After the children have completed the sheet, discuss the activity with the class. You may decide to do this either before or after marking the activity. Use the *Discussion questions* as a springboard. For each activity there are questions that have been designed to cater for higher attaining (↑) and lower attaining (↓) pupils.

Marking

- Mark the sheet with the whole class, either before or after the discussion. You may wish the children to mark their own sheet or to swap with someone next to them. However, if you are using the activity as an assessment tool then you may decide to mark the sheets yourself at a later stage.

Revisiting an activity

- Repeat an activity with the class at a later stage in the year. Children can compare how they performed on the task the second time round.
- You may like to alter the activity slightly by changing one or two of the instructions.

Collins New Primary Maths: Speaking and Listening and assessment

Collins New Primary Maths: Speaking and Listening activities may be used with the whole class or with groups of children as an assessment activity. Linked to the topic that is being studied at present, *Collins New Primary Maths: Speaking and Listening* will provide you with an indication of how well the children have understood the objectives being covered as well as how their listening skills are developing. The *Collins New Primary Maths: Speaking and Listening* assessment sheet on page 11 may be used to record how well the children have understood the objectives covered in the activity.

Collins New Primary Maths: Speaking and Listening assessment sheet

YEAR
CLASS
TEACHER

/ Not understood ∠ Developing an understanding Δ Completely understood

	ACTIVITY																													
NAME	1	2	3	4	5	6	7	8	9	10	11	12	13	14	15	16	17	18	19	20	21	22	23	24	25	26	27	28	29	30

Foundation Using and applying mathematics

- Talk about, recognise and recreate simple patterns.

Resources

Provide each child with the following:

- a copy of Activity 1 pupil sheet
- a pencil

Key words

continue the pattern next last

Say to the children:

Listen carefully.

I am going to tell you some things to do.

I will say them only once, so listen very carefully.

Do only the things you are told to do and nothing else.

If you make a mistake, cross it out. Do not use an eraser.

There are 7 parts to this activity.

Answers

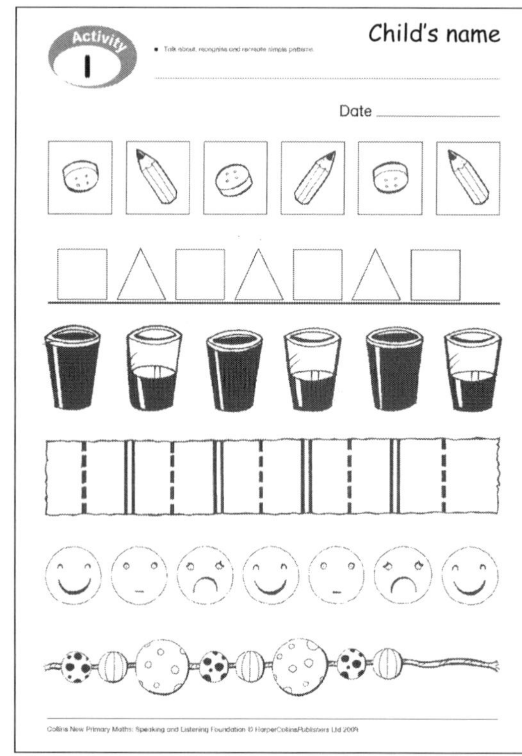

The activity

1. Look at the buttons and the pencils.
   Continue the pattern by drawing the next object in the box.
2. Look at the shapes.
   Continue the pattern by drawing the next two shapes on the line.
3. Look at the glasses of juice.
   Continue the pattern by colouring the last glass.
4. Look at the wallpaper.
   Continue the pattern by drawing the next strip on the paper.
5. Look at the faces.
   Continue the pattern by drawing the next face.
6. Look at the beads.
   Continue the pattern by drawing the next two beads on the string.
7. Write your name at the top of the sheet.

Discussion questions

- ↓ Look at the buttons and pencils. What object did you draw? (pencil)
- ↓ Continue this pattern. Clap, clap, pause, clap, clap, pause…
- ■ Look at all the faces. What face did you draw? (happy face) If you were to continue the pattern what would the next two faces show? (straight face, sad face)
- ■ Which pattern was the easiest/hardest? Why?
- ↑ Who can come out to the easel and draw a pattern for us? Who can come out and continue (*child's name*) pattern?
- ↑ Continue this pattern. Clap, clap, click, click, pause, clap, clap, click, click, pause…

- Talk about, recognise and recreate simple patterns.

Date ______________

    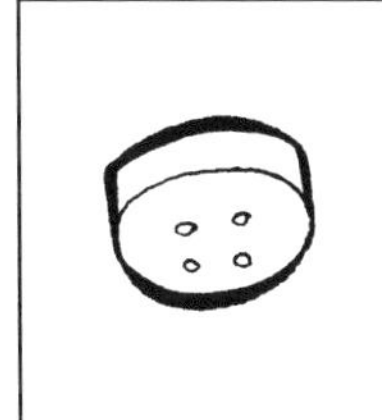 

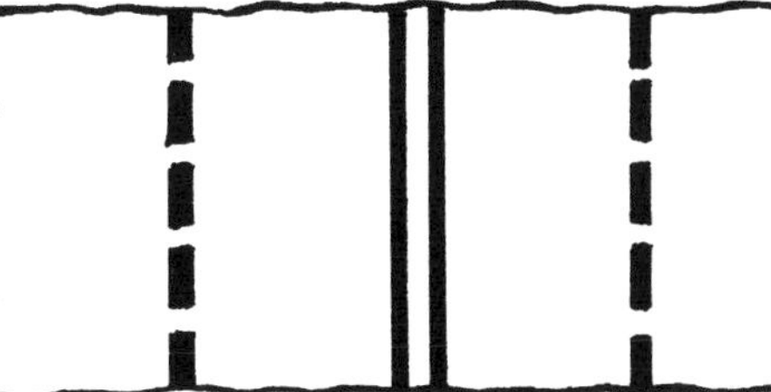 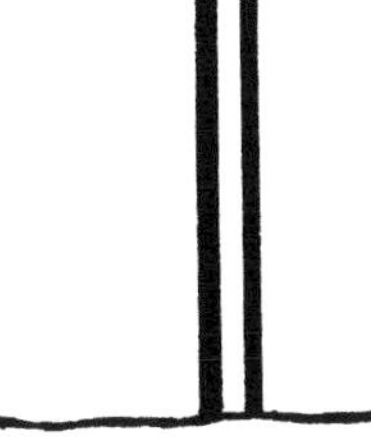   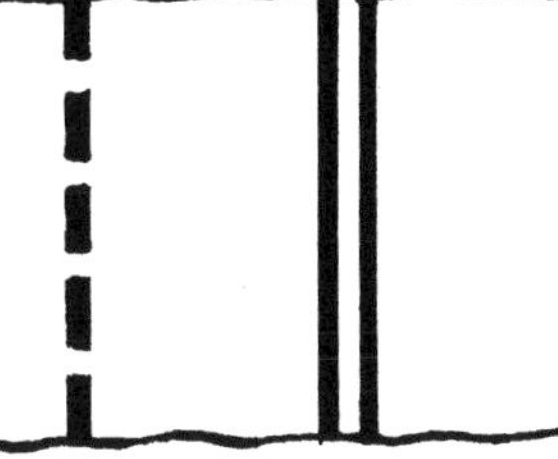

      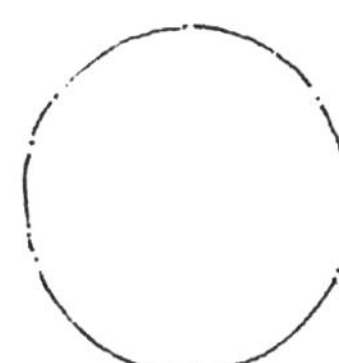

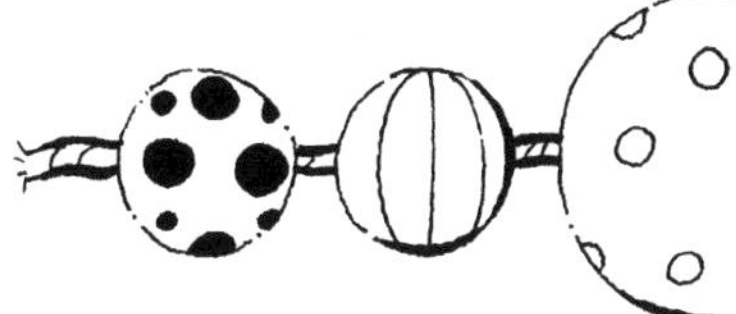 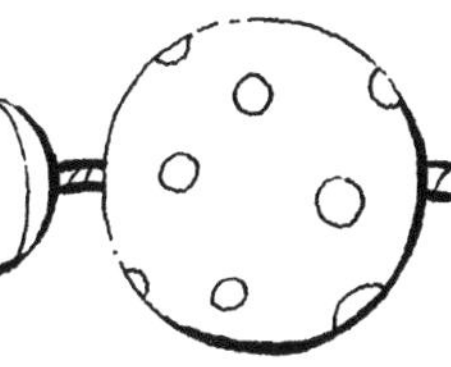 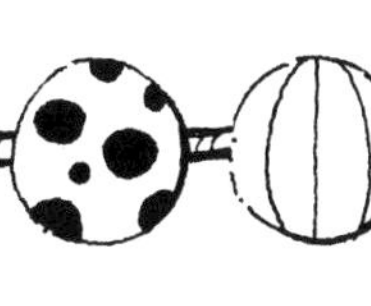 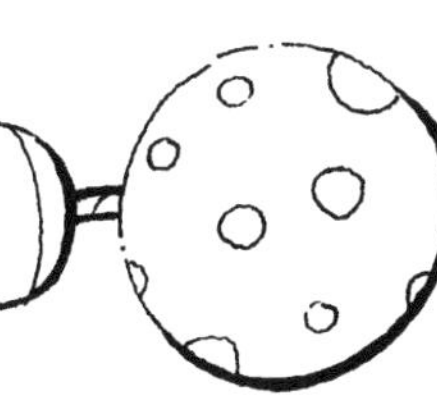

Collins New Primary Maths: Speaking and Listening Foundation © HarperCollins*Publishers* Ltd 2009

Foundation Using and applying mathematics

- Sort objects, making choices and justifying decisions.

Resources

Provide each child with the following:

- a copy of Activity 2 pupil sheet
- a red and blue coloured pencil or crayon

Key words

match

Say to the children:

Listen carefully.

I am going to tell you some things to do.

I will say them only once, so listen very carefully.

Do only the things you are told to do and nothing else.

If you make a mistake, cross it out. Do not use an eraser.

There are 5 parts to this activity.

The activity

1. Look at the knife.
   Colour the knife red.
   Now colour red the object that goes with the knife.
2. Look at the fruit.
   Draw a cross through all the fruit.
3. Look at the shapes.
   Colour all the shapes blue.
4. Look at the shoes.
   Draw a line to match each pair of shoes.
5. Look at the coins.
   Write your name next to each coin.

Answers

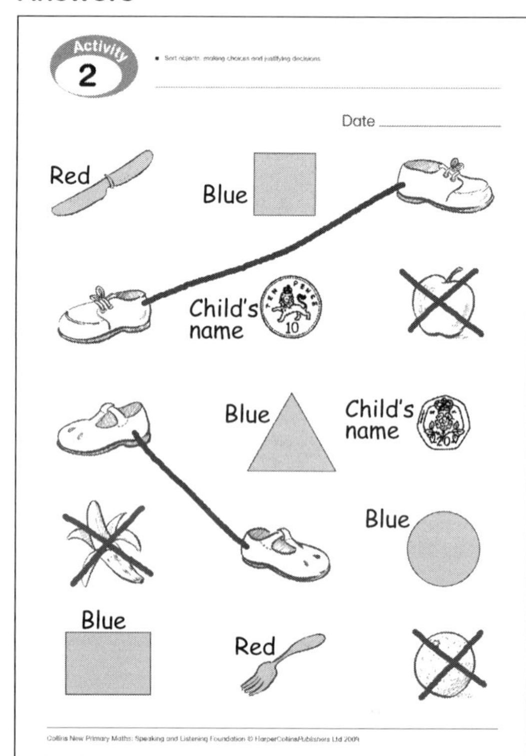

Discussion questions

↓ Describe for me the pairs of shoes that match.

↓ How many times did you write your name on the sheet? (2)
What did you write your name next to? (coins)

■ Look at all the objects you drew a cross through. How many are there? (3)
Why do they all have a cross through them? (They are all fruit.)

■ Which objects did you colour blue? (shapes)

↑ Look at the objects you coloured red. Why are they coloured red? (Because they go together, a knife goes with a fork.) What other object that is not on the sheet goes with a knife and a fork? (a spoon)

↑ Tell me some other objects that go together. Why do they go together?

- Sort objects, making choices and justifying decisions.

Date ___________

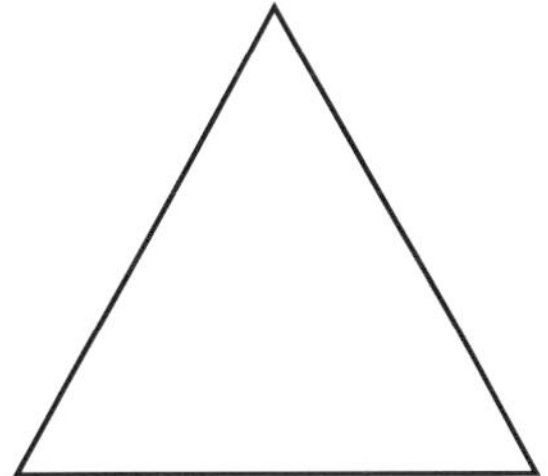

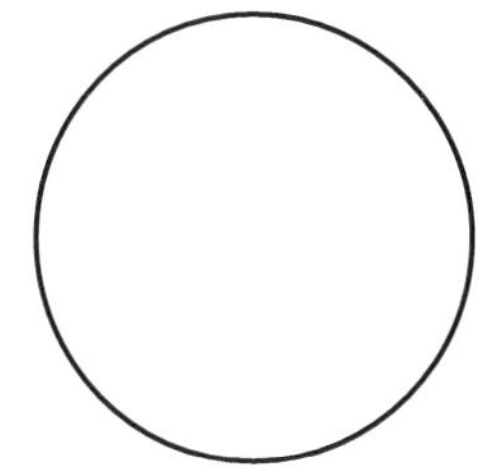

Collins New Primary Maths: Speaking and Listening Foundation © HarperCollins*Publishers* Ltd 2009

Activity 3

Foundation Using and applying mathematics

■ Use developing mathematical ideas and methods to solve practical problems.

Resources

Provide each child with the following:

■ a copy of Activity 3 pupil sheet

■ a pencil

Key words

zero, one, two…ten altogether how many? pair under above

Say to the children:

Listen carefully.

I am going to tell you some things to do.

I will say them only once, so listen very carefully.

Do only the things you are told to do and nothing else.

If you make a mistake, cross it out. Do not use an eraser.

There are 8 parts to this activity.

The activity

1. Look at Cinderella's coach. How many wheels would there be if Cinderella had two coaches? Write that number in the box under Cinderella's coach.
2. Look at Puss in Boots. If Puss has two pairs of boots how many boots is that altogether? Write that number in the box next to Puss in Boots.
3. Look at Goldilocks and the Three Bears. If Goldilocks and the Three Bears invite another three bears for a bowl of porridge how many bowls of porridge are needed? Write that number in the box under the bears.
4. Look at Snow White and the Seven Dwarfs. If Snow White and two of the dwarfs go off to the garden, how many dwarfs will be left in the house? Write that number in the box under the dwarfs.
5. Look at Little Red Riding Hood, the wolf, grandmother and the woodcutter. How many ears do they have altogether? Write that number in the box under Little Red Riding Hood.
6. Look at Old Mother Hubbard's cupboard. If Old Mother Hubbard went and bought four bones and two dog biscuits how many things would she have to put in the cupboard? Write that number in the box under the dog.
7. Write your name above Old Mother Hubbard's cupboard.
8. Look at Humpty Dumpty. If Humpty fell off the wall and broke into eight pieces, how many pieces would each of the King's men have to pick up to try to put Humpty back together again? Write that number in the box under Humpty Dumpty.

Answers

Discussion questions

↓ How many boots does Puss in Boots have altogether? (4)

↓ What number did you write in the box under Goldilocks and the Three Bears? (7)

■ If Snow White stayed in the cottage and five of the dwarfs went off to the garden, how many people would be left in the house? (3)

■ How many pieces would each of the King's men have to pick up to try to put Humpty back together again? (2) How did you work this out?

↑ How many feet do Snow White and the Seven Dwarfs have altogether? (16) How did you work this out?

↑ How many of the King's men helped to put Humpty Dumpty back together again? (4) If another four men came to help them how many would that be altogether? (8) Now how many pieces would each of the King's men have to pick up to try to put Humpty back together again? (1)

- Use developing mathematical ideas and methods to solve practical problems.

Date ______________

Foundation Using and applying mathematics

- Use developing mathematical ideas and methods to solve practical problems (in the context of money).

Resources

Provide each child with the following:
- a copy of Activity 4 pupil sheet
- a red, blue, green and yellow coloured pencil or crayon

Key words

coins pee pence penny pound above

Say to the children:

Listen carefully.

I am going to tell you some things to do.

I will say them only once, so listen very carefully.

Do only the things you are told to do and nothing else.

If you make a mistake, cross it out. Do not use an eraser.

There are 7 parts to this activity.

The activity

1. Find all the two pence coins.
   Colour all the two pence coins red.
2. Find all the ten pence coins.
   Colour all the ten pence coins blue.
3. Find the fifty pence coin.
   Write your name above the fifty pence coin.
4. Find all the one-penny coins.
   Colour all the one-penny coins green.
5. Find all the one pound coins.
   Draw a cross through all the one pound coins.
6. Find all the five pence coins.
   Draw a ring around each of the five pence coins.
7. Find all the twenty pence coins.
   Colour all the twenty pence coins yellow.

Answers

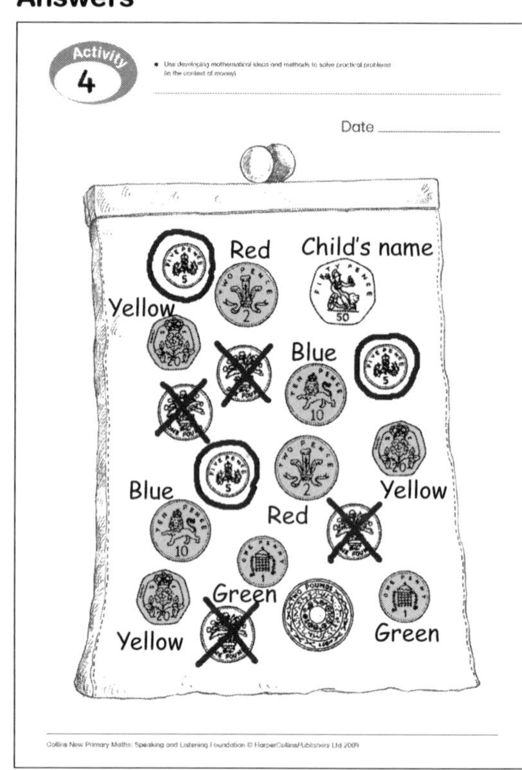

Discussion questions

- ↓ Which coins did you colour yellow? (20p)
- ↓ Which coin on the sheet did you do nothing to? (£2)
- ■ How many five pence coins are on the sheet? (3)
- ■ Which coin on the sheet would you like to have? Why?
- ↑ How many ten pence coins are there? (2) How much money is this altogether? (20p)
- ↑ Would you rather have all the coins you coloured blue or all the coins you drew a ring around? (All the coins coloured blue.) Why? (The three five pence coins with a ring around them total fifteen pence and the two ten pence coins coloured blue total twenty pence.)

- Use developing mathematical ideas and methods to solve practical problems (in the context of money).

Date ____________________

Activity 5

Foundation **Counting and understanding number**

- Say and use the number names in order in familiar contexts.

Resources

Provide each child with the following:

- a copy of Activity 5 pupil sheet
- a pencil

Key words

zero, one, two…twenty before next twice largest

Say to the children:

Listen carefully.

I am going to tell you some things to do.

I will say them only once, so listen very carefully.

Do only the things you are told to do and nothing else.

If you make a mistake, cross it out. Do not use an eraser.

There are 6 parts to this activity.

The activity

1. One, two, three, four, five.
   Draw a cross through the number that comes next.
   I will say the numbers again. One, two, three, four, five.
2. One, two, four, five.
   Draw a ring around the number I missed out.
   I will say the numbers again. One, two, four, five.
3. Sixteen, seventeen, eighteen, eighteen, nineteen.
   Draw a line under the number I said twice.
   I will say the numbers again. Sixteen, seventeen, eighteen, eighteen, nineteen.
4. Write your name under the number that comes before six.
5. Eight, nine, ten, eleven.
   Draw a flower around the number that comes next.
   I will say the numbers again. Eight, nine, ten, eleven.
6. Draw a box around the largest number on the sheet.

Answers

Discussion questions

- ↓ Tell me a number that is on the sheet. Point to the number.
- ↓ Point to the number sixteen.
- What is the smallest number on the sheet? (0)
- Where did you write your name? (Under number 5)
- ↑ Tell me a teens number. (12–19 inclusive)
- ↑ Tell me a number that is not on the sheet.
  Can you write it on the easel?

■ Say and use the number names in order in familiar contexts.

Date ____________

2 15 3

20

17 8

14 18 1

9 6 16 4

11 13

10 0

19 12

5 7

 © HarperCollins*Publishers* Ltd 2009

Activity 6

Foundation **Counting and understanding number**

■ Count aloud in ones.

Resources

Provide each child with the following:

- a copy of Activity 6 pupil sheet
- a red, blue, green and yellow coloured pencil or crayon

Key words

zero, one, two…twenty   count on   count back

Say to the children:

Listen carefully.

I am going to tell you some things to do.

I will say them only once, so listen very carefully.

Do only the things you are told to do and nothing else.

If you make a mistake, cross it out. Do not use an eraser.

There are 6 parts to this activity.

The activity

1. Start at six, hold the number six in your head and count on three. What number do you come to? Colour that balloon red.
2. Start at fourteen, hold the number fourteen in your head and count on five. What number do you come to? Colour that balloon green.
3. Start at seven, hold the number seven in your head and count back four. What number do you come to? Write your name on that balloon.
4. Start at five, hold the number five in your head and count back five. What number do you come to? Colour that balloon blue.
5. Start at nine, hold the number nine in your head and count on six. What number do you come to? Colour that balloon yellow.
6. Start at twenty, hold the number twenty in your head and count back four. What number do you come to? Draw a cross through that balloon.

Answers

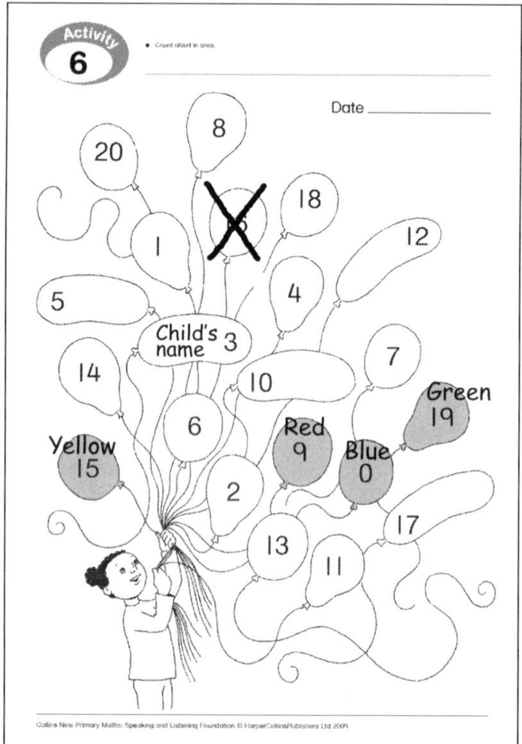

Discussion questions

↓ Tell me a number that you have coloured. (0, 9, 15, 19)

↓ (*Pointing to a number on the sheet.*) What number is this?

■ When you count forwards, which number is one before six? (5)

■ Count backwards in twos. Which number comes after fourteen? (12)

↑ How many do you need to count on from fifteen to reach nineteen? (4)

↑ How many do you need to count back from eleven to reach eight? (3)

- Count aloud in ones.

Date ____________

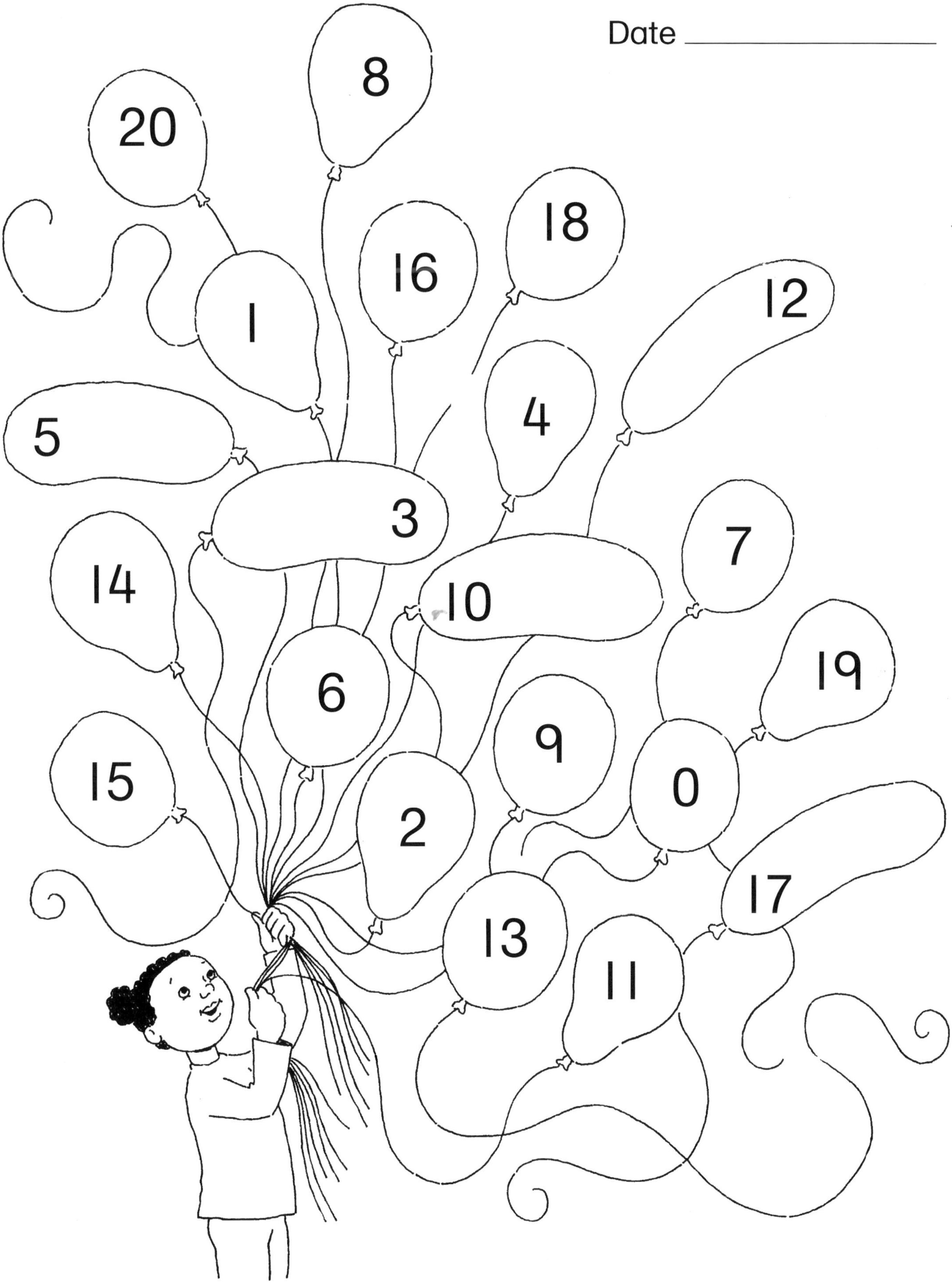

8 20 18 16 12 1 5 4 3 14 7 10 19 6 15 2 9 0 17 13 11

Collins New Primary Maths: Speaking and Listening Foundation © HarperCollins*Publishers* Ltd 2009

Activity 7

Foundation Counting and understanding number

- Count reliably up to 10 everyday objects.

Resources

Provide each child with the following:

- a copy of Activity 7 pupil sheet
- a pencil

Key words

zero, one, two…twenty under

Say to the children:

Listen carefully.

I am going to tell you some things to do.

I will say them only once, so listen very carefully.

Do only the things you are told to do and nothing else.

If you make a mistake, cross it out. Do not use an eraser.

There are 6 parts to this activity.

The activity

1. Look at the keys. Draw a box around eight keys.
2. Look at the bells. Draw a ring around six bells.
3. Look at the pencils. Draw a cross through three pencils.
4. Look at the flags. Draw a line under four flags.
5. Write your name at the top of the sheet.
6. Look at the stars. Count how many stars there are and draw a ring around that number at the bottom of the sheet.

Answers

Discussion questions

- ↓ How many bells did you circle? (6)
- ↓ How many flags are underlined? (4)
- ■ Which number did you draw a ring around? (5)
- ■ How many pencils do not have a cross through them? (7)
- ↑ If you were to draw a line under three more flags, how many flags would that be altogether? (7)
- ↑ If I were to take away three keys from inside the box, how many would be left inside the box? (5)

■ Count reliably up to 10 everyday objects.

Date ______________

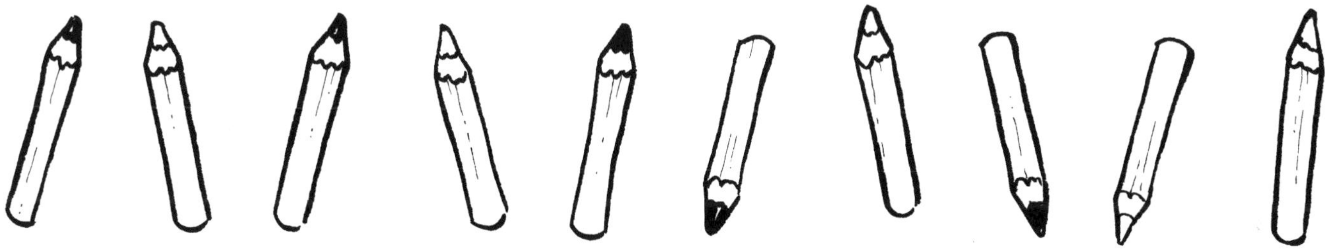

0 1 2 3 4 5 6 7 8 9 10

Foundation Counting and understanding number

■ Recognise numerals 1 to 9.

Resources

Provide each child with the following:
- a copy of Activity 8 pupil sheet
- a pencil
- a ruler

Key words

zero, one, two…twenty

Say to the children:

Listen carefully.
I am going to tell you some things to do.
I will say them only once, so listen very carefully.
Do only the things you are told to do and nothing else.
If you make a mistake, cross it out. Do not use an eraser.
There are 13 parts to this activity.

The activity

1. Draw a line from number 5 to number 12.
2. Draw a line from number 9 to number 11.
3. Draw a line from number 15 to number 8.
4. Draw a line from number 11 to number 0.
5. Draw a line from number 17 to number 12.
6. Draw a line from number 10 to number 18.
7. Draw a line from number 19 to number 20.
8. Draw a line from number 11 to number 7.
9. Draw a line from number 15 to number 10.
10. Draw a line from number 1 to number 17.
11. Draw a line from number 7 to number 9.
12. Draw a line from number 0 to number 19.
13. Write your name inside the kite.

Answers

Discussion questions

- ↓ How many birds saw the kite? (8)
- ↓ Point to the number seventeen.
- ■ What numbers on the sheet did you not use to draw your kite? (2, 6, 13, 14, 16)
- ■ What is the smallest/largest number on the sheet? (0/20)
- ↑ Tell me a number that is not on the sheet. Can you write it on the easel?
- ↑ (*Write the number twenty-four on the easel.*) What number is this?

- Recognise numerals 1 to 9.

Date ______________

2
7
11
4
16
6
9
0
13
17
5
19
1
12
14
10
8
20
18
15
3

Collins New Primary Maths: Speaking and Listening Foundation © HarperCollins*Publishers* Ltd 2009

Foundation Counting and understanding number

■ Recognise (and record) numerals 1 to 9.

Resources

Provide each child with the following:

- a copy of Activity 9 pupil sheet
- a pencil

Key words

zero, one, two…twenty above

Say to the children:

Listen carefully.

I am going to tell you some things to do.

I will say them only once, so listen very carefully.

Do only the things you are told to do and nothing else.

If you make a mistake, cross it out. Do not use an eraser.

There are 8 parts to this activity.

The activity

1. Look at the footballer. Write the number six on his shirt.
2. Look at the door. Write the number fifteen on the door.
3. Look at the bus. Write the number three on the bus.
4. Look at the coin. Write the number ten on the coin.
5. Look at the racing car. Write the number two on the racing car.
6. Look at the flower. Write your name above the flower.
7. Look at the train. Write the number fourteen on the train.
8. Look at the stamp. Write the number nineteen on the stamp.

Answers

Discussion questions

↓ Which number did you write on the footballer's shirt? (6)

↓ Which object did you not write a number on? (ball)

■ Tell me a number between zero and twenty that you did not write down. Can you write it on the easel?

■ Come and write the number eleven on the easel.

↑ Tell me a number greater than twenty. Can you write it on the easel?

↑ Give me a number between the number that is on the train and the number on the stamp. (15, 16, 17 or 18)

■ Recognise (and record) numerals 1 to 9.

Date ______________

Foundation Counting and understanding number

■ Use language such as 'more' or 'less' to compare two numbers.

Resources

Provide each child with the following:

- a copy of Activity 10 pupil sheet
- a pencil
- a coloured pencil or crayon

Key words

zero, one, two…twenty more most great/greater/greatest less least fewer/fewest small/smaller/smallest

Say to the children:

Listen carefully.

I am going to tell you some things to do.

I will say them only once, so listen very carefully.

Do only the things you are told to do and nothing else.

If you make a mistake, cross it out. Do not use an eraser.

There are 9 parts to this activity.

The activity

1. Look at the vases of flowers. Colour the vase that has fewer flowers in it.
2. Look at the baskets of apples. Draw a ring around the basket that has more apples in it.
3. Look at the button. Write a number greater than six on the button.
4. Look at the ball. Write a number smaller than fifteen on the ball.
5. Look at the leaves with the ladybirds on them. Draw a cross through the leaf that has the greatest number of ladybirds on it.
6. Look at the leaves with the ladybirds on them again. Colour the leaf that has the least number of ladybirds on it.
7. Look at the pots of pencils. Draw a ring around the pot with the fewest number of pencils in it.
8. Look at the pots of pencils again. Colour the pot with the most pencils in it.
9. Write your name at the bottom of the sheet.

Answers

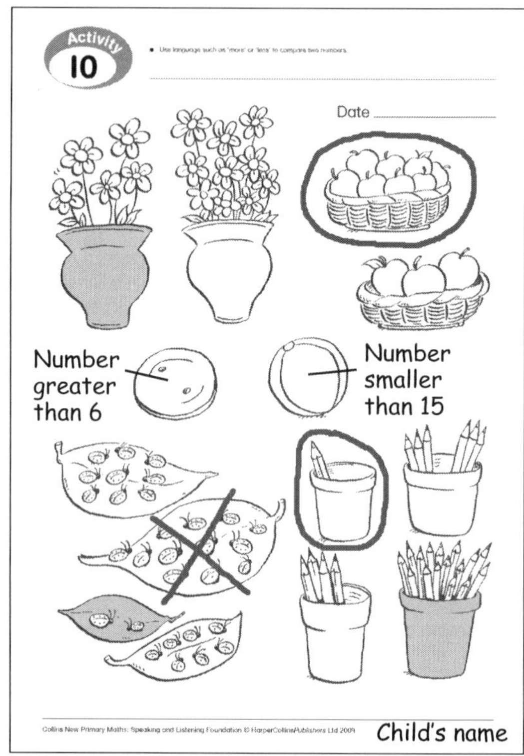

Discussion questions

↓ What number did you write on the button? (any number greater than 6) Can you write it on the easel?

↓ Point to the pot with the most pencils in it.

■ What is another word for less? (e.g. smaller, fewer)

■ How many apples are there altogether in both baskets? (11)

↑ What is the opposite of more? (less)

↑ Look at the baskets of apples. How many more would you need to put in the basket with only three apples to make it the same as the other basket? (5)

Activity 10

■ Use language such as 'more' or 'less' to compare two numbers.

Date ____________

Collins New Primary Maths: Speaking and Listening Foundation © HarperCollins*Publishers* Ltd 2009

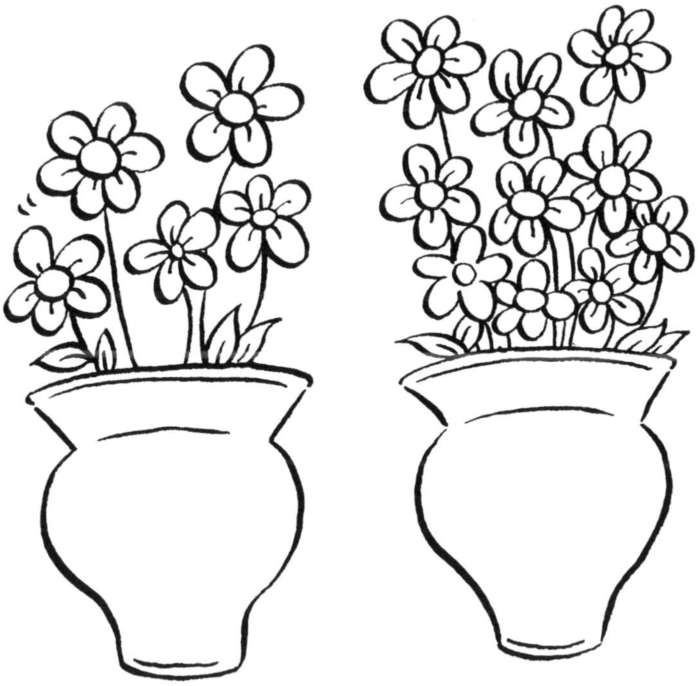

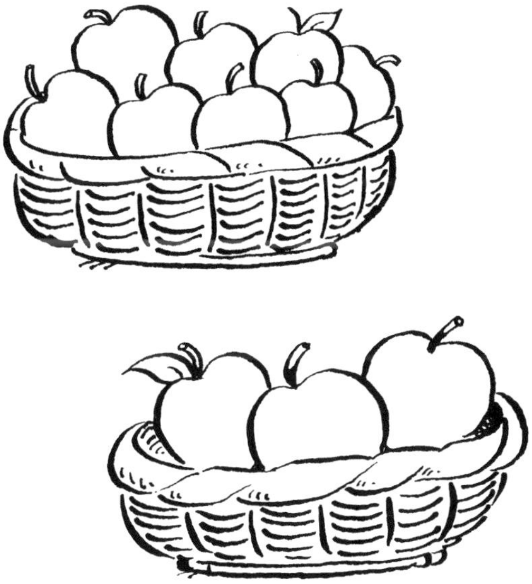

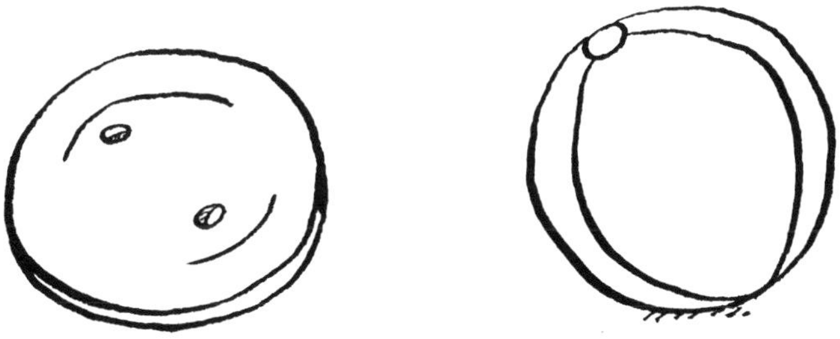

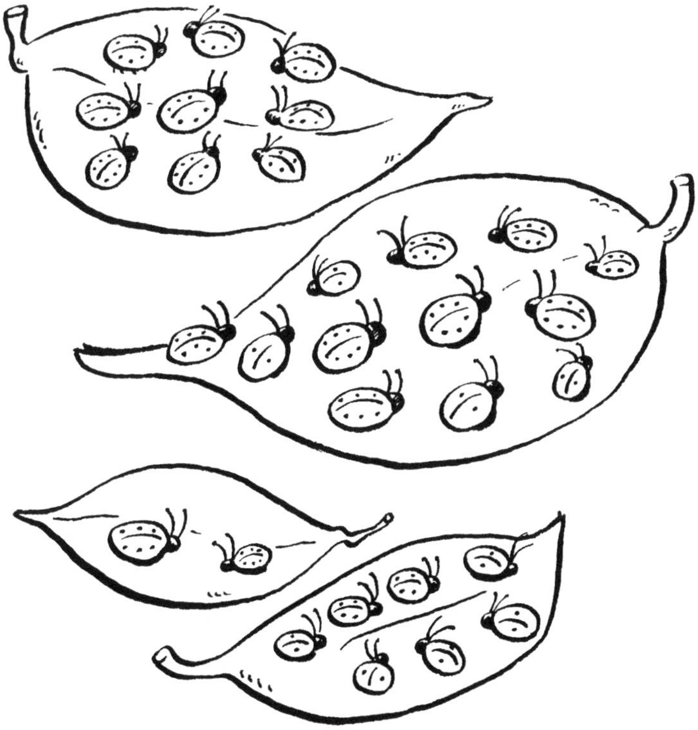

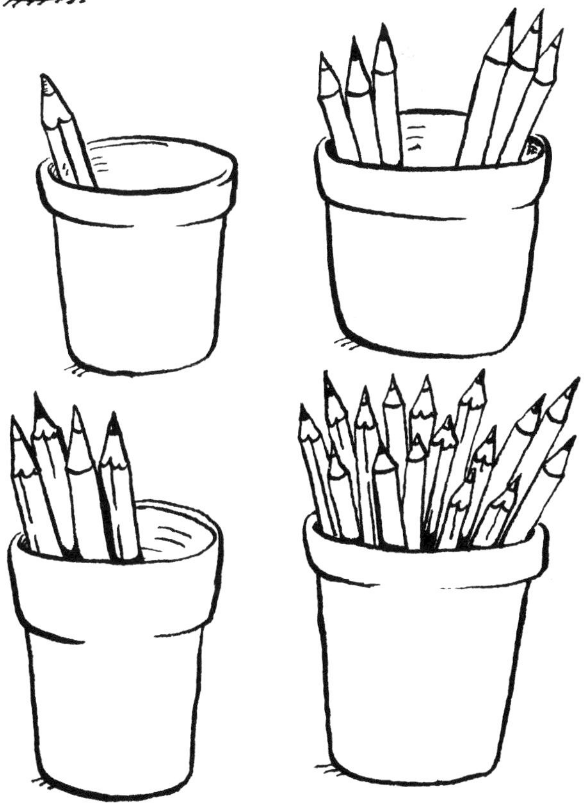

Foundation Counting and understanding number

- Compare two numbers (and say a number that lies between them).

Resources

Provide each child with the following:

- a copy of Activity 11 pupil sheet
- a red, blue, green and yellow coloured pencil or crayon

Key words

zero, one, two…twenty between above

Say to the children:

Listen carefully.

I am going to tell you some things to do.

I will say them only once, so listen very carefully.

Do only the things you are told to do and nothing else.

If you make a mistake, cross it out. Do not use an eraser.

There are 9 parts to this activity.

The activity

For each instruction think of a number track.

1. Which number lies between six and eight? Find that number and colour that card red.
2. Which number lies between twelve and fourteen? Find that number and colour that card green.
3. Which number lies between four and six? Find that number and colour that card yellow.
4. Which number lies between ten and twelve? Find that number and colour that card blue.
5. Which number lies between three and five? Find that number and write your name above that card.
6. Which number lies between eleven and thirteen? Find that number and colour that card green.
7. Which number lies between five and seven? Find that number and colour that card yellow.
8. Which number lies between eight and ten? Find that number and colour that card red.
9. Which number lies between seven and nine? Find that number and colour that card blue.

Answers

Discussion questions

- ↓ Which two numbers did you colour red? (7 and 9) Which number lies between them? (8)
- ↓ Tell me a number smaller than/greater than four? (0, 1, 2, 3/5, 6, 7...)
- ■ Does ten lie between six and thirteen? (yes) What other numbers lie between six and thirteen? (7, 8, 9, 11, 12)
- ■ Which number lies between eleven and thirteen? (12) What colour is that number? (green)
- ↑ Look at the two numbers on the cards at the top of the sheet. Tell me all the numbers that lie between them. (15, 16 and 17)
- ↑ Choose two of the numbers that are not coloured and tell me all the numbers that lie between them.

■ Compare two numbers (and say a number that lies between them).

Date ______________

14 18

11 20 4 6

15 7 13 10 19

12 9 16 5

1 2 8 3 17

Collins New Primary Maths: Speaking and Listening Foundation © HarperCollins*Publishers* Ltd 2009

Activity 12

Foundation Counting and understanding number

- Use the number names in order.
- Order a set of numbers.

Resources

Provide each child with the following:

- a copy of Activity 12 pupil sheet
- a pencil

Key words

zero, one, two…twenty order small/smaller/smallest large/larger/largest underneath

Say to the children:

Listen carefully.

I am going to tell you some things to do.

I will say them only once, so listen very carefully.

Do only the things you are told to do and nothing else.

If you make a mistake, cross it out. Do not use an eraser.

There are 5 parts to this activity.

The activity

1. Look at the birthday cakes with the number candles on top. Put these cakes in order, starting with the smallest, by drawing the candles on the cakes underneath.
2. Look at the birthday cards with the numbers on them. Put these cards in order, starting with the smallest, by writing the numbers on the cards underneath.
3. Write your name at the top of the sheet.
4. Look at the balloons with the numbers on them. Put these balloons in order, starting with the smallest, by writing the numbers on the balloons underneath.
5. Look at the presents with the numbers on them. Put these presents in order, smallest to largest, by writing the numbers on the presents underneath.

Answers

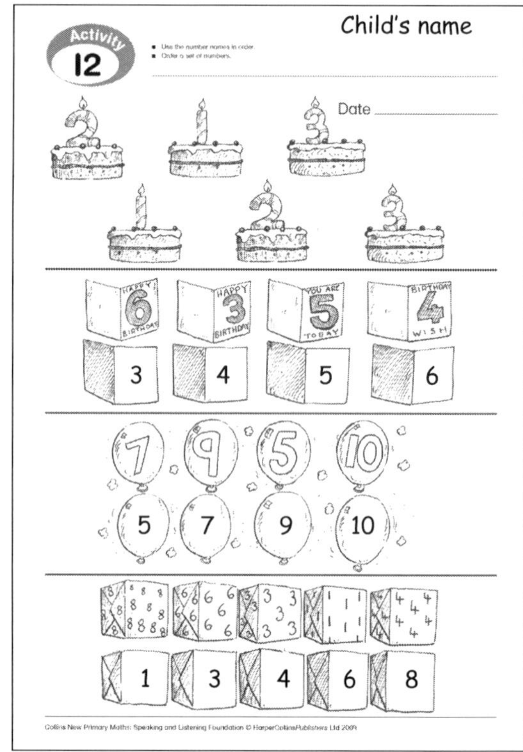

Discussion questions

- Look at the candles you drew on the birthday cakes. Which number is first? (1)
- Look at the sheets of wrapping paper. What is the largest number on the wrapping paper? (8)
- Tell me in order, smallest to largest, the numbers on the birthday cards? (3, 4, 5, 6)
- Look at the birthday cards you drew. Which number lies between three and five? (4)
- Tell me in order, largest to smallest, the numbers on the balloons? (10, 9, 7, 5)
- Five, seven, eleven, two. Tell me these numbers in order, smallest to largest. Five, seven, eleven, two (2, 5, 7, 11)

- Use the number names in order.
- Order a set of numbers.

Date ______________

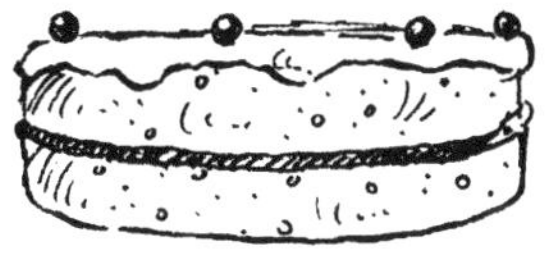
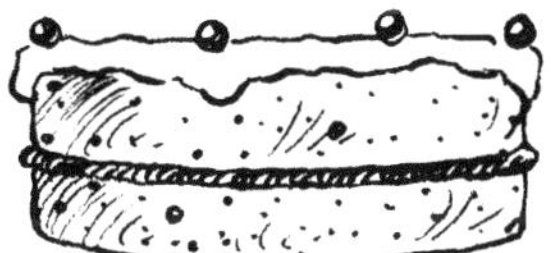
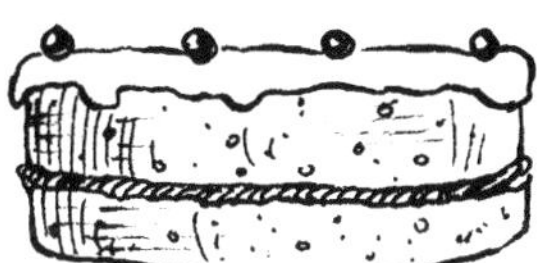

Collins New Primary Maths: Speaking and Listening Foundation © HarperCollins*Publishers* Ltd 2009

Foundation Counting and understanding number

- Use ordinal numbers in different contexts.

Resources

Provide each child with the following:

- a copy of Activity 13 pupil sheet
- a coloured pencil or crayon

Key words

first, second, third, fourth, fifth last vehicle

Say to the children:

Listen carefully.

I am going to tell you some things to do.

I will say them only once, so listen very carefully.

Do only the things you are told to do and nothing else.

If you make a mistake, cross it out. Do not use an eraser.

There are 9 parts to this activity.

The activity

1. Look at the car park. Colour the second motorbike.
2. Look at the car park again. Draw a line under the last car.
3. Look at the car park again. Write your name under the first car.
4. Look at the petrol station. Draw a cross through the third car.
5. Look at the petrol station again. Colour the second truck.
6. Look at the petrol station again. Draw a ring around the last motorbike.
7. Look at the traffic lights. Draw a line under the fourth car.
8. Look at the traffic lights again. Draw a cross through the first truck.
9. Look at the traffic lights again. Colour the fifth car.

Answers

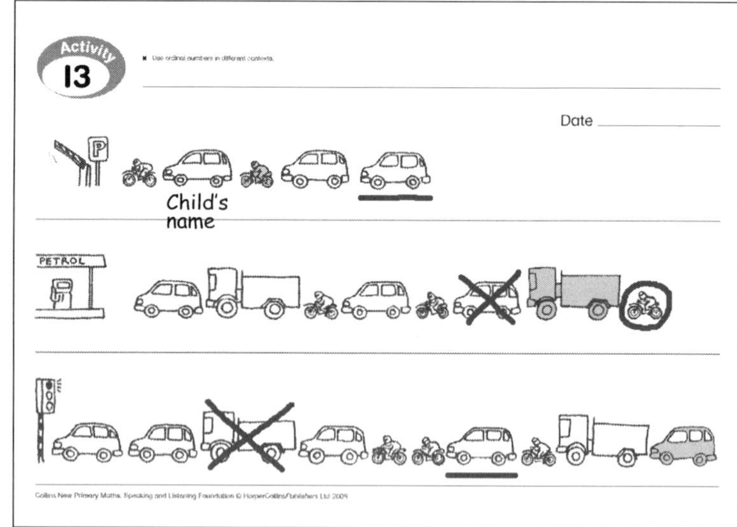

Discussion questions

- Look at the car park. How many motorbikes are there? (2)
- How many vehicles are waiting at the traffic lights? (10)
- Look at the car park. What positions do the cars come in the queue? (2nd, 4th and 5th)
- Look at the traffic lights. What is the eighth vehicle? (motorbike)
- Look at the petrol station. What is the second last vehicle? (truck)
- Look at the petrol station. What vehicle is between the second and third car? (motorbike)

- Use ordinal numbers in different contexts.

Date ____________

Collins New Primary Maths: Speaking and Listening Foundation © HarperCollins*Publishers* Ltd 2009

Activity 14

Foundation Knowing and using number facts

■ Select two groups of objects to make a given total of objects.

Resources

Provide each child with the following:

- a copy of Activity 14 pupil sheet
- a coloured pencil or crayon

Key words

zero, one, two…ten make total

Say to the children:

Listen carefully.

I am going to tell you some things to do.

I will say them only once, so listen very carefully.

Do only the things you are told to do and nothing else.

If you make a mistake, cross it out. Do not use an eraser.

There are 6 parts to this activity.

Answers

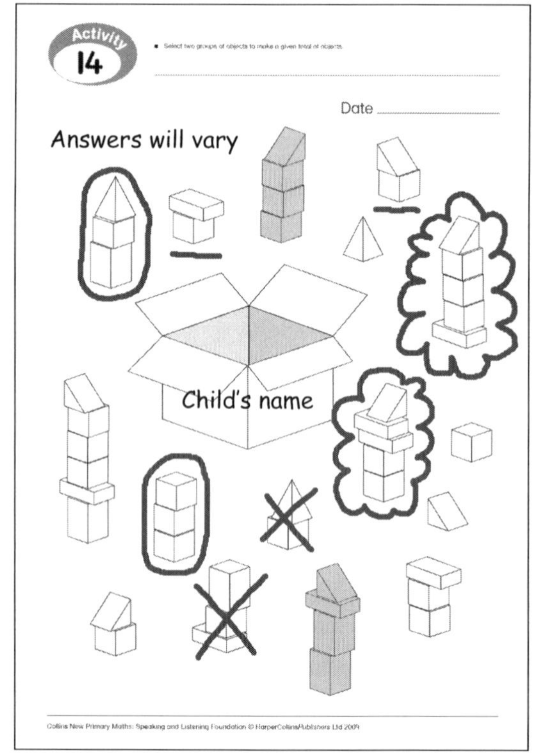

The activity

1. Find two towers that together make six. Draw a ring around each tower.
2. Find two towers that together make four. Draw a line under each tower.
3. Find two towers that together make eight. Colour each tower.
4. Find two towers that total five. Draw a cross through each tower.
5. Find two towers that together make ten. Draw a flower around each tower.
6. Write your name on the box.

Discussion questions

↓ Which two towers did you colour? How many blocks is that altogether? (8)

↓ Point to a tower of six blocks. Point to a tower with less than six blocks.

■ Which two towers make ten? Are there another two towers that total ten? Are there any more?

■ Find the tower of five cubes. Which other tower will make eight blocks altogether? (3)

↑ Look at the towers you did nothing to. How many blocks are there altogether? (14)

↑ Tell me which three towers total eight. (e.g. 3 + 3 + 2) Are there others?

- Select two groups of objects to make a given total of objects.

Date ______________

Activity 15

Foundation Knowing and using number facts

- Find one more or one less than a number from 1 to 10.

Resources

Provide each child with the following:

- a copy of Activity 15 pupil sheet
- a red, blue, green and yellow coloured pencil or crayon

Key words

zero, one, two…twelve more less

Say to the children:

Listen carefully.

I am going to tell you some things to do.

I will say them only once, so listen very carefully.

Do only the things you are told to do and nothing else.

If you make a mistake, cross it out. Do not use an eraser.

There are 7 parts to this activity.

Answers

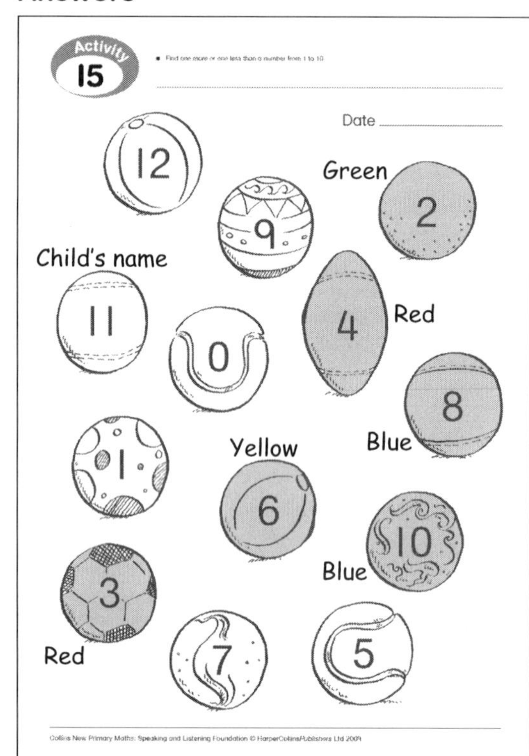

The activity

1. Find the number one more than seven. Colour that ball blue.
2. Find the number one more than two. Colour that ball red.
3. Find the number one less than five. Colour that ball red.
4. Find the number one less than three. Colour that ball green.
5. Find the number one more than nine. Colour that ball blue.
6. Find the number one less than seven. Colour that ball yellow.
7. Find the number one more than ten. Write your name above that ball.

Discussion questions

- ↓ How many numbers did you colour? (6) What was the largest/smallest number you coloured? (10/2)
- ↓ What number is one less than nine? (8)
- ■ Look at the numbers you coloured. How many numbers are less than 10? (5) What are these numbers? (2, 3, 4, 6 and 8)
- ■ What are the two numbers you coloured red? (3 and 4) What do you notice about these two numbers? (3 is one less than 4; 4 is one more than 3)
- ↑ Look at all the numbers you coloured. Tell me the numbers in order smallest to largest. (2, 3, 4, 6, 8, 10)
- ↑ What is two more than/less than six? (8/4)

Activity
15

■ Find one more or one less than a number from 1 to 10.

Date ____________

12
9
2
11
0
4
8
1
6
10
3
7
5

Collins New Primary Maths: Speaking and Listening Foundation © HarperCollinsPublishers Ltd 2009

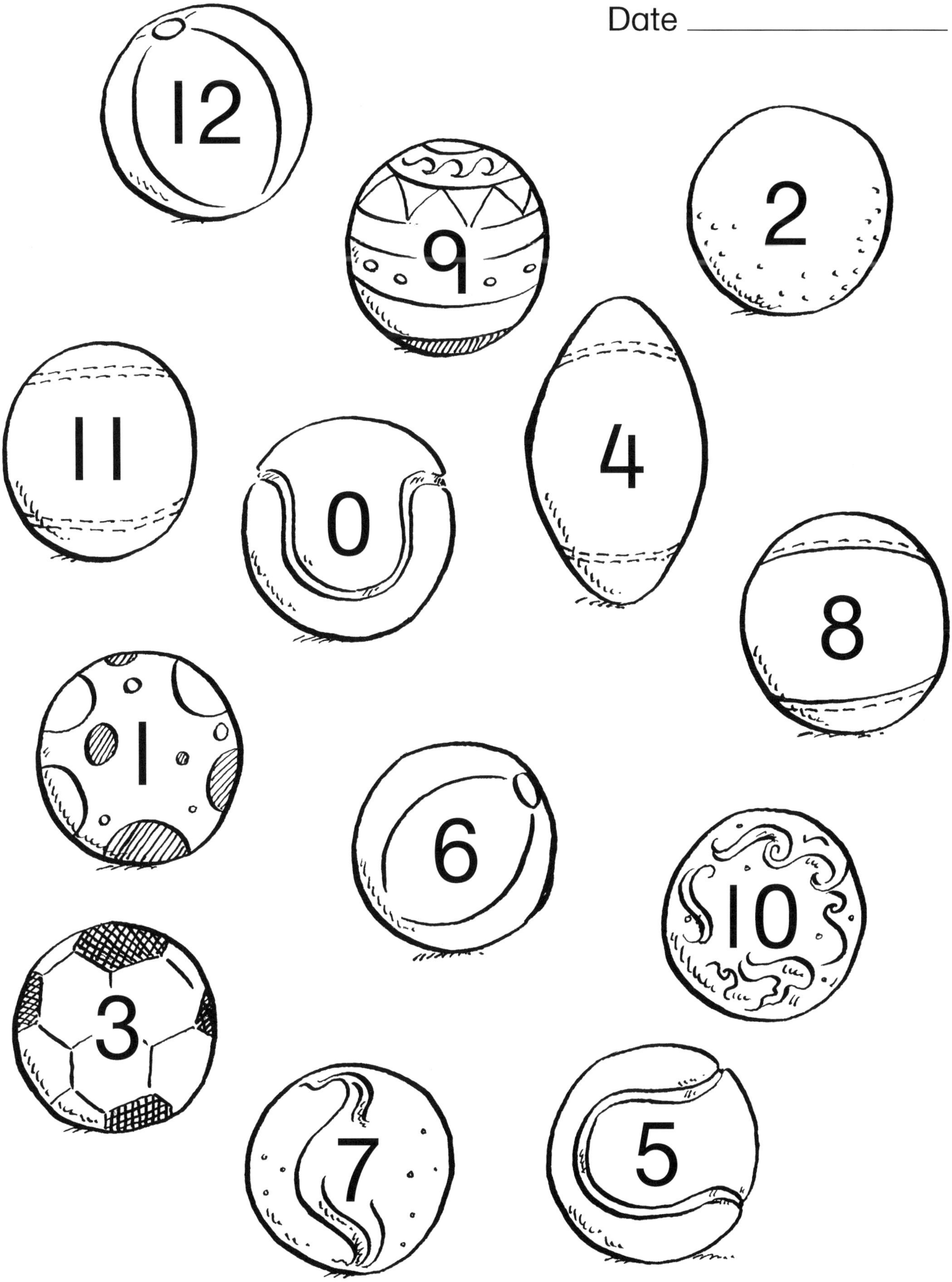

Activity 16

Foundation Calculating

- In practical activities and discussion begin to use the vocabulary involved in adding.
- Begin to relate addition to combining two groups of objects.

Resources

Provide each child with the following:

- a copy of Activity 16 pupil sheet
- a pencil

Key words

zero, one, two…ten add altogether total sum

Say to the children:

Listen carefully.

I am going to tell you some things to do.

I will say them only once, so listen very carefully.

Do only the things you are told to do and nothing else.

If you make a mistake, cross it out. Do not use an eraser.

There are 6 parts to this activity.

The activity

1. Look at the baskets of oranges. How many oranges are there altogether? Write this number on the large orange at the bottom of the sheet.
2. Look at the baskets of bananas. How many bananas are there in total? Write this number on the large banana at the bottom of the sheet.
3. Look at the baskets of pears. How many pears are there altogether? Write this number on the large pear at the bottom of the sheet.
4. Look at the baskets of watermelons. Count up all the watermelons. Write this number on the large watermelon at the bottom of the sheet.
5. Look at the baskets of apples. What is the sum of all the apples? Write this number on the large apple at the bottom of the sheet.
6. Write your name on the label on the box at the bottom of the sheet.

Answers

Discussion questions

- How many apples are there altogether? (10)
- The greengrocer has seven of one fruit. Which fruit is that? (banana)
- Does the greengrocer have more oranges or bananas? (oranges) How many more? (2)
- Which fruit does the greengrocer have the least of? (watermelons)
- If the greengrocer sold three bananas how many would he have left? (4)
- A customer asked the greengrocer for ten pears. Does he have enough? (No) How many more pears does the greengrocer need? (2)

- In practical activities and discussion begin to use the vocabulary involved in adding.
- Begin to relate addition to combining two groups of objects.

Date ___________________

Collins New Primary Maths: Speaking and Listening Foundation © HarperCollins*Publishers* Ltd 2009

Foundation Calculating

- In practical activities and discussion begin to use the vocabulary involved in subtracting.
- Begin to relate subtraction to 'taking away'.

Resources

Provide each child with the following:

- a copy of Activity 17 pupil sheet
- a pencil

Key words

zero, one, two…ten take away how many are left?

Say to the children:

Listen carefully.

I am going to tell you some things to do.

I will say them only once, so listen very carefully.

Do only the things you are told to do and nothing else.

If you make a mistake, cross it out. Do not use an eraser.

There are 7 parts to this activity.

The activity

1. Look at the bears. Count how many there are. Take away four bears. How many bears are left? Write that number on the toy-box.
2. Look at the toy soldiers. Count how many there are. Take away three toy soldiers. How many toy soldiers are left? Write that number on the toy-box.
3. Look at the dolls. Count how many there are. Take away two dolls. How many dolls are left? Write that number on the toy-box.
4. Look at the toy car. Write your name on the car.
5. Look at the robots. Count how many there are. Take away five robots. How many robots are left? Write that number on the toy-box.
6. Look at the clowns. Count how many there are. Take away one clown. How many clowns are left? Write that number on the toy-box.
7. Look at the cowboys. Count how many there are. Take away three cowboys. How many cowboys are left? Write that number on the toy-box.

Answers

Discussion questions

- ↓ We started with seven of one toy and ended up with three. Which toy was that? (bears)
- ↓ Now that we have taken some of our toys away, which toy do we have the least of/most of? (robots/cowboys)
- ■ If there were six robots and five of them went away, how many would be left? (1)
- ■ Did we start with more toy soldiers or robots? (toy soldiers) How many more toy soldiers were there than robots? (2)
- ↑ How many cowboys were there to start with? (9) How many did you take away? (3) How many were left? (6) How many would be left if you took away another four cowboys? (2)
- ↑ How many dolls and clowns did we start with? (9) How many dolls and clowns do we have now? (6) How many dolls and clowns have we taken away? (3)

- In practical activities and discussion begin to use the vocabulary involved in subtracting.
- Begin to relate subtraction to 'taking away'.

Date ________________

 © HarperCollins*Publishers* Ltd 2009

Foundation Calculating

- In practical activities and discussion begin to use the vocabulary involved in adding and subtracting.
- (Separate (partition) a given number of objects into two groups.)

Resources

Provide each child with the following:
- a copy of Activity 18 pupil sheet
- a coloured pencil or crayon

Key words

zero, one, two…ten count

Say to the children:

Listen carefully.

I am going to tell you some things to do.

I will say them only once, so listen very carefully.

Do only the things you are told to do and nothing else.

If you make a mistake, cross it out. Do not use an eraser.

There are 6 parts to this activity.

The activity

1. Count the biscuits.
   Now imagine putting these biscuits onto two plates.
   Draw the biscuits on the two plates.
2. Count the flowers.
   Now imagine putting these flowers into two vases.
   Draw the flowers in the two vases.
3. Count the coins.
   Now imagine putting these coins into two purses.
   Draw the coins in the two purses.
4. Count the beads.
   Now imagine putting these beads onto two necklaces.
   Draw the beads on the two necklaces.
5. Count the sheep.
   Now imagine putting these sheep into two pens.
   Draw the sheep in the two pens.
6. Write your name at the top of the sheet.

Answers

Discussion questions

- ↓ How many sheep are there? (4) How did you share the sheep between the two pens?
- ↓ Were there more beads or biscuits? (beads) How many more? (2)
- ■ How many flowers are there? (8) If I put three flowers in one vase, how many would I have to put into the other vase? (5)
- ■ How many coins are there? (6) How did you share the coins between the two purses? How else could you have shared out the coins? Is there another way? Are there any others?
- ↑ How could you share out ten sweets between two children? How else could you share out the sweets? Is there another way? Are there any other ways?
- ↑ How many flowers were there? (8) How did you share the flowers between the two vases? How could you share them out between three vases? How else could you share them out? Any other ways?

Activity 18

- In practical activities and discussion begin to use the vocabulary involved in adding and subtracting.
- (Separate (partition) a given number of objects into two groups.)

Date ____________________

Collins New Primary Maths: Speaking and Listening Foundation © HarperCollins*Publishers* Ltd 2009

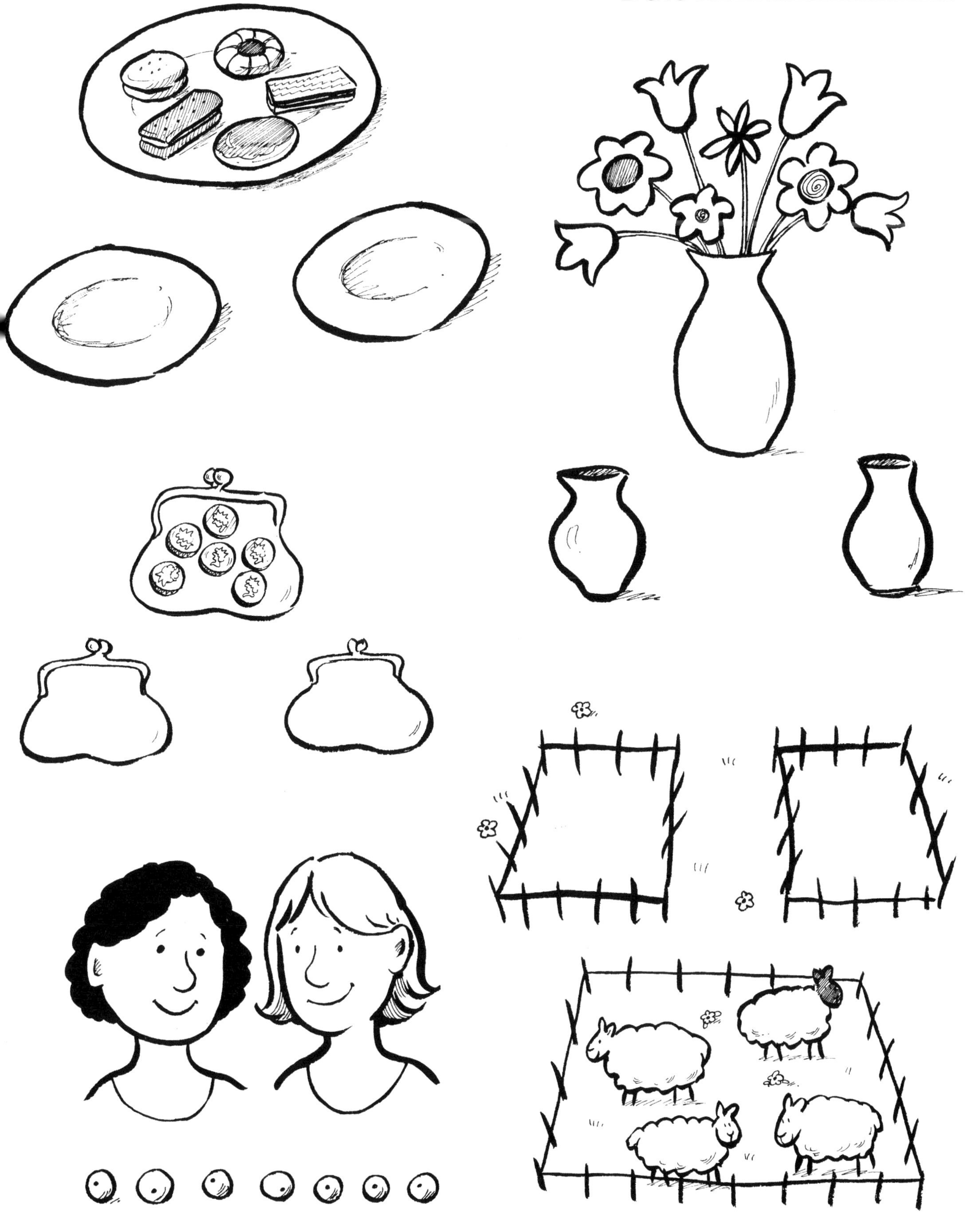

Foundation Calculating

- In practical activities and discussion begin to use the vocabulary involved in adding and subtracting.
- Begin to find out how many have been removed from a larger group of objects by counting up from a number.

Resources

Provide each child with the following:

- a copy of Activity 19 pupil sheet
- a pencil

Key words

zero, one, two…ten

Say to the children:

Listen carefully.

I am going to tell you some things to do.

I will say them only once, so listen very carefully.

Do only the things you are told to do and nothing else.

If you make a mistake, cross it out. Do not use an eraser.

There are 7 parts to this activity.

The activity

1. Look at the flower. There were seven petals on the flower. How many have fallen off? Write that number on the vase.
2. Look at the bag of sweets. There were seven sweets in the bag. How many have been eaten? Write that number on the bag.
3. Look at the plate of chips. There were ten chips on the plate. How many have been eaten? Write that number on the plate.
4. Look at the apple tree. There were nine apples on the tree. How many have been picked? Write that number on the tree trunk.
5. Look at the bookshelf. There were eight books on the shelf. How many have gone? Write that number on the bookshelf.
6. Look at the egg carton. There were six eggs in the carton. How many have been used? Write that number on the lid of the carton.
7. Write your name at the bottom of the sheet.

Answers

Discussion questions

- ↓ What was the largest/smallest number you wrote down? (6/1)
- ↓ There were eight of one object to start with. Which object was this? (books)
- ■ Look at the bag of sweets. How many sweets were there to start with? (7) How did you work out how many had been eaten?
- ■ Two groups of objects had the same number to start with. Which objects were these? (flowers and sweets) How did you work out how many had gone?
- ↑ Of all the objects on the sheet, which object was there the most of to start with? (chips) How did you work out how many had been eaten?
- ↑ Look at the apple tree. How many would have been picked if there were twelve apples on the tree to start with? (4)

- In practical activities and discussion begin to use the vocabulary involved in adding and subtracting.
- Begin to find out how many have been removed from a larger group of objects by counting up from a number.

Date ____________________

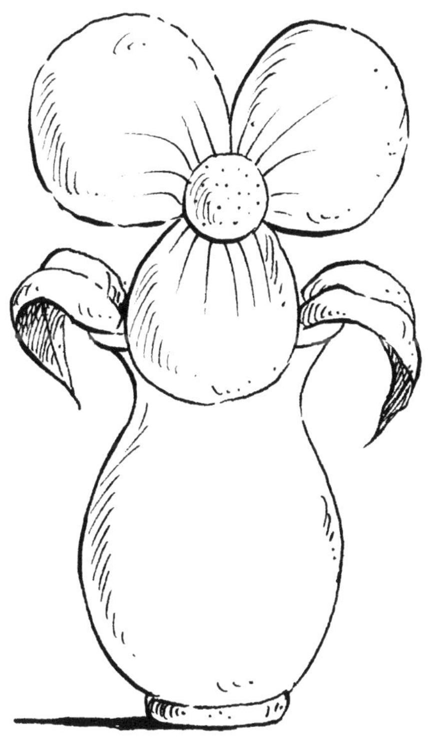

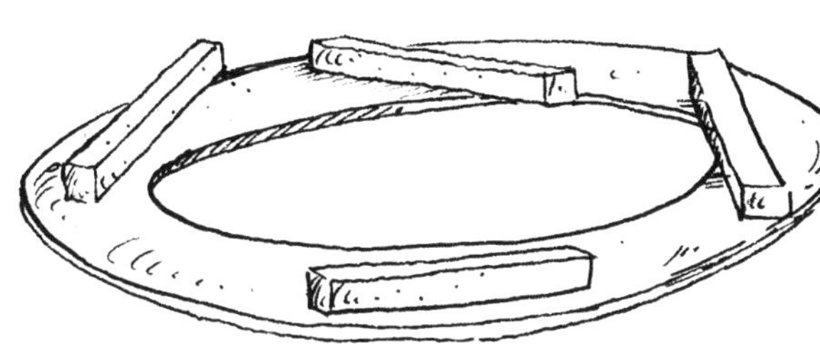

Foundation Calculating

- In practical activities and discussion begin to use the vocabulary involved in adding and subtracting.
- Work out by counting how many more are needed to make a larger number.

Resources

Provide each child with the following:

- a copy of Activity 20 pupil sheet
- a pencil

Key words

zero, one, two…ten how many more?

Say to the children:

Listen carefully.

I am going to tell you some things to do.

I will say them only once, so listen very carefully.

Do only the things you are told to do and nothing else.

If you make a mistake, cross it out. Do not use an eraser.

There are 7 parts to this activity.

The activity

1. Count the cars. Six children want to ride the cars. How many more cars are needed? Write that number next to the cars.
2. Count the balls. Ten children want to play with the balls. How many more balls are needed? Write that number next to the balls.
3. Count the skipping ropes. Seven children want to play with the skipping ropes. How many more skipping ropes are needed? Write that number next to the ropes.
4. Count the bicycles. Eight children want to ride the bicycles. How many more bicycles are needed? Write that number next to the bicycles.
5. Count the swings. Three children want to play on the swings. How many more swings are needed? Write that number next to the swings.
6. Count the hoops. Ten children want to play with the hoops. How many more hoops are needed? Write that number inside one of the hoops.
7. Write your name at the top of the sheet.

Answers

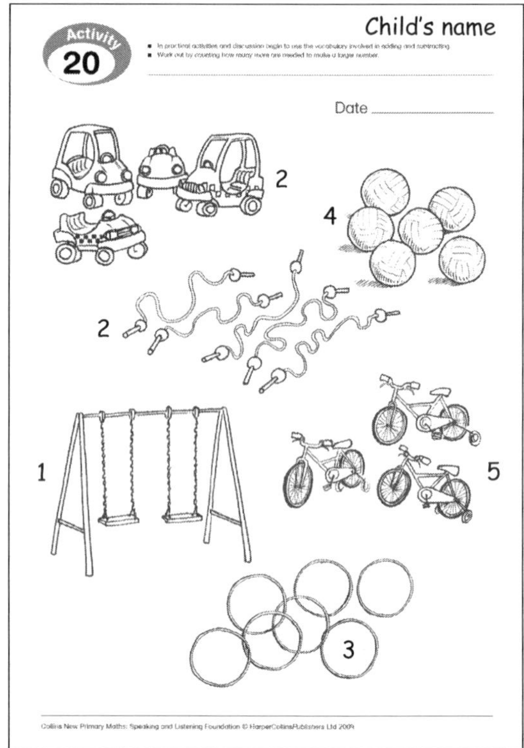

Discussion questions

- Are there more hoops or swings? (hoops) How many more? (5)
- How many more balls than swings are there? (4)
- How many more skipping ropes would be needed so that there would be enough for ten children? (5)
- How many bikes and balls are there altogether? (9)
- How many more cars are needed so that there is the same number of cars as hoops? (3)
- How many cars, ropes and swings are there altogether? (11)

- In practical activities and discussion begin to use the vocabulary involved in adding and subtracting.
- Work out by counting how many more are needed to make a larger number.

Date ________________

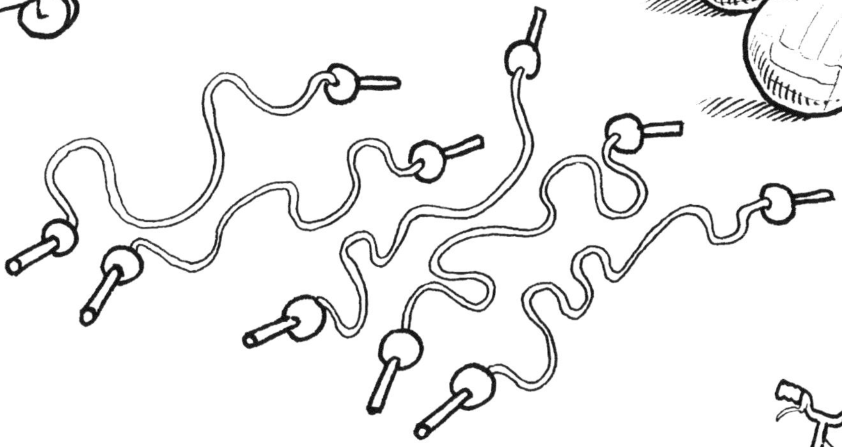

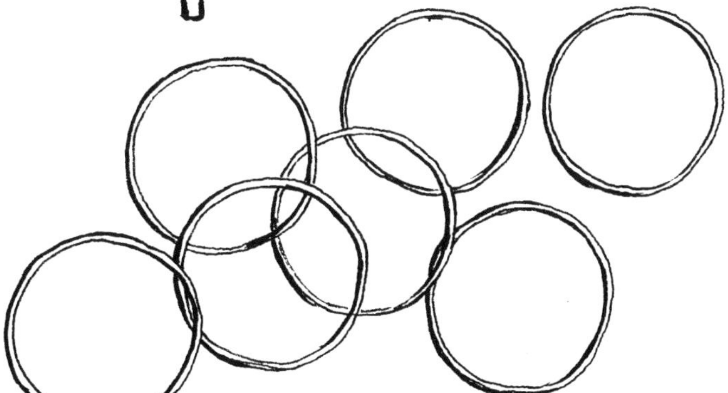

 © HarperCollins*Publishers* Ltd 2009

Activity 21

Foundation Understanding shape

■ Use language such as 'circle' or 'bigger' to describe the shape and size of flat shapes.

Resources

Provide each child with the following:

- a copy of Activity 21 pupil sheet
- a red, blue, green and yellow coloured pencil or crayon

Key words

small/smaller/smallest large/larger/largest square rectangle triangle circle

Say to the children:

Listen carefully.

I am going to tell you some things to do.

I will say them only once, so listen very carefully.

Do only the things you are told to do and nothing else.

If you make a mistake, cross it out. Do not use an eraser.

There are 7 parts to this activity.

The activity

1. Colour the smallest rectangle red.
2. Colour the largest circle blue.
3. Write your name inside the largest square.
4. Colour the smallest triangle yellow.
5. Draw a line from the largest circle to the smallest square.
6. Count how many triangles there are.
   Write this number inside the smallest circle.
7. Colour the largest rectangle green.

Answers

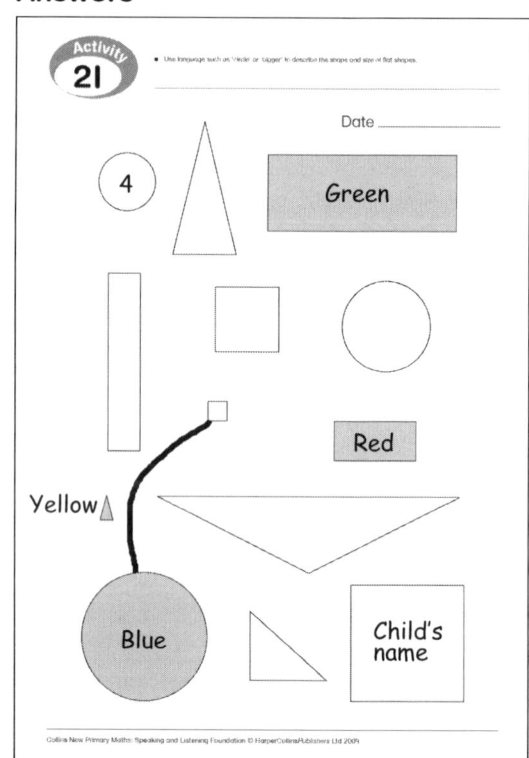

Discussion questions

↓ Describe the shape that you coloured blue? (largest circle)

↓ Which two shapes did you draw a line between? (largest circle and smallest square)

■ How many triangles are there? (4)

■ How many shapes are on the sheet? (13)
How many of those are squares and rectangles? (6)

↑ Describe a triangle for me. What is the difference between a square and a triangle?

↑ Did anyone colour the wrong shape? Which shape was that? Why did you do that?

Activity 21

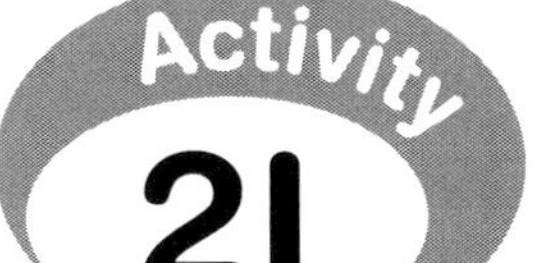

- Use language such as 'circle' or 'bigger' to describe the shape and size of flat shapes.

Date ______________

Collins New Primary Maths: Speaking and Listening Foundation © HarperCollins*Publishers* Ltd 2009

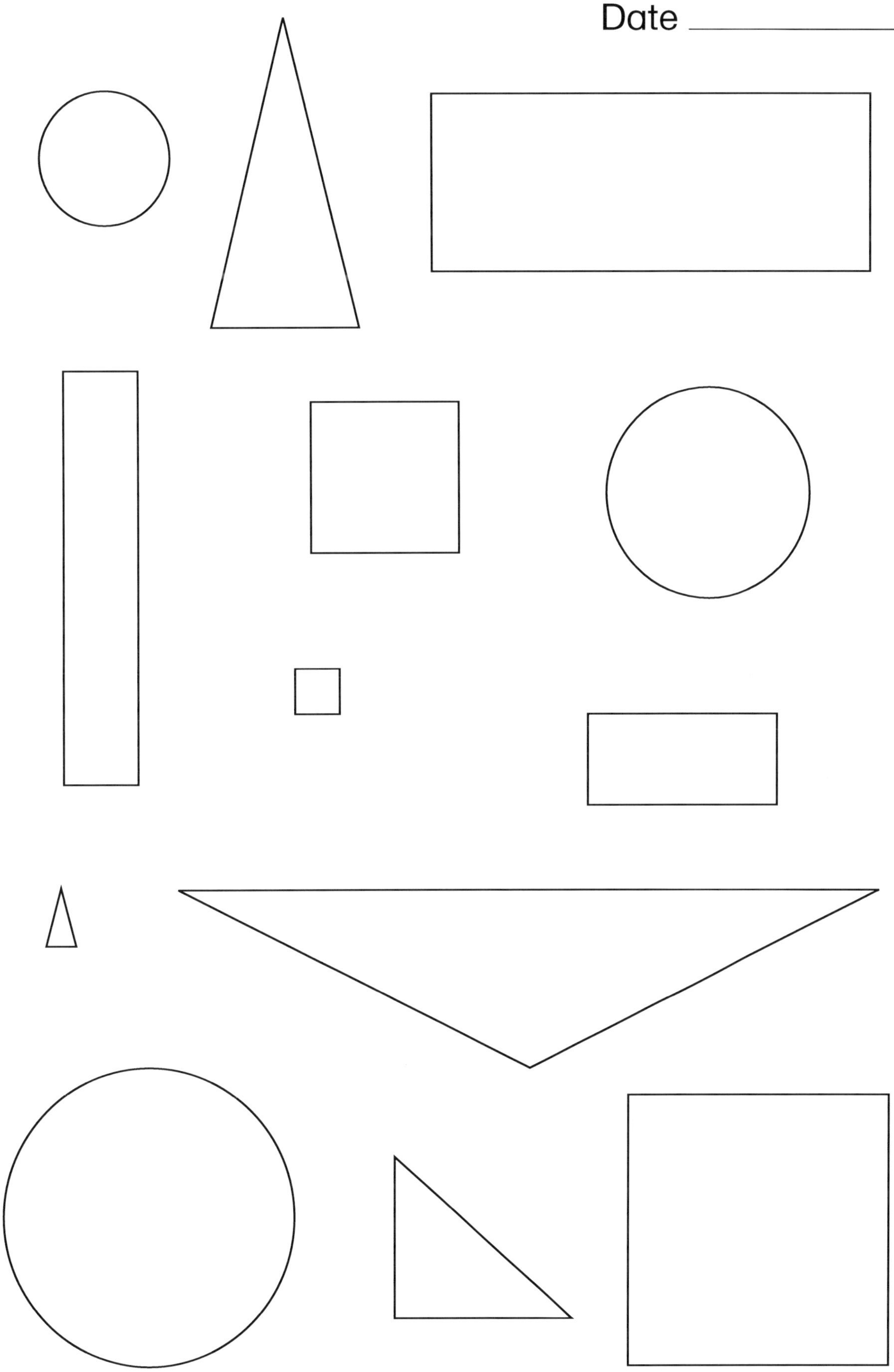

Activity 22

Foundation Understanding shape

- Use language such as 'bigger' to describe the shape and size of solid shapes.

Resources

Provide each child with the following:

- a copy of Activity 22 pupil sheet
- a red, blue, green and yellow coloured pencil or crayon

Key words

small/smaller/smallest large/larger/largest cube pyramid cone sphere

Say to the children:

Listen carefully.

I am going to tell you some things to do.

I will say them only once, so listen very carefully.

Do only the things you are told to do and nothing else.

If you make a mistake, cross it out. Do not use an eraser.

There are 7 parts to this activity.

The activity

1. Colour the largest cube green.
2. Colour the smallest cone yellow.
3. Colour the smallest sphere red.
4. Write your name under the largest pyramid.
5. Draw a line from the smallest cube to the largest sphere.
6. Colour the largest cone blue.
7. Count how many cones there are.
   Write this number under the smallest pyramid.

Answers

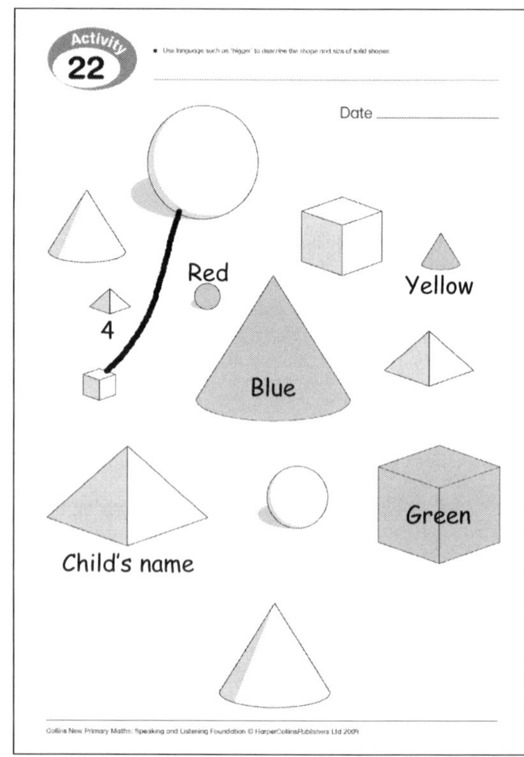

Discussion questions

↓ Describe the shape that you coloured red. (smallest sphere)

↓ What two shapes did you draw a line between? (smallest cube and largest sphere)

■ How many cones are there? (4)

■ Choose a shape on the sheet and describe it to me.

↑ Describe a pyramid for me.

↑ Look at the shape at the bottom of the sheet and the shape you coloured blue.
What is the same/different about these two shapes? (both cones/the blue cone is larger)

■ Use language such as 'bigger' to describe the shape and size of solid shapes.

Date ______________

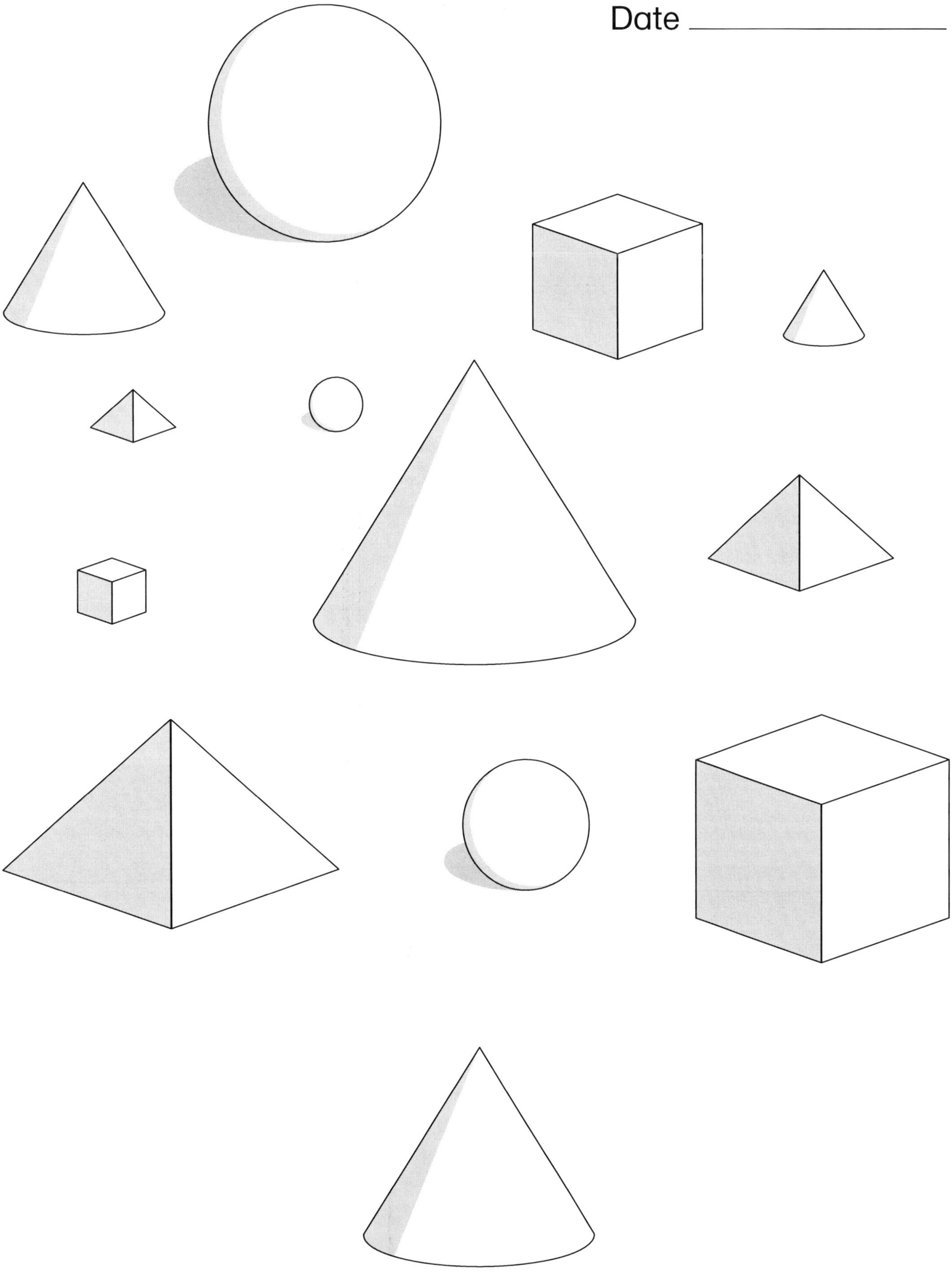

Activity 23

Foundation Understanding shape

- Use familiar objects and common shapes to create and recreate patterns.

Resources

Provide each child with the following:

- a copy of Activity 23 pupil sheet
- a red, blue, green, yellow and black coloured pencil or crayon

Key words

zero, one, two…ten

Say to the children:

Listen carefully.

I am going to tell you some things to do.

I will say them only once, so listen very carefully.

Do only the things you are told to do and nothing else.

If you make a mistake, cross it out. Do not use an eraser.

There are 7 parts to this activity.

The activity

1. Look at the carpet drawn on your sheet.
   Write your name at the top of the sheet.
2. Colour blue the shape that has the number one written on it.
3. Colour green the shape that has the number four written on it.
4. Colour yellow the shape that has the number five written on it.
5. Colour black the shape that has the number ten written on it.
6. Colour red the shape that has the number three written on it.
7. Look at the line down the centre of the carpet.
   Using your coloured pencils/crayons colour all of the other shapes so that the colour of the shape that is on one side of the line is the same as the colour of the shape on the other side.

Answers

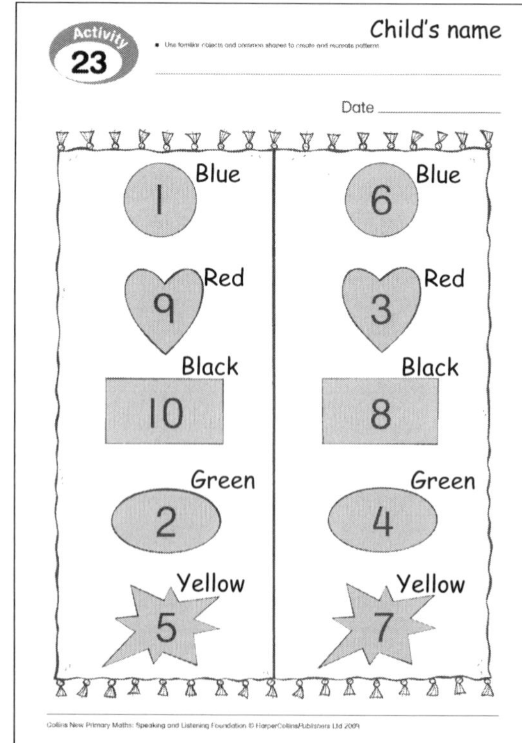

Discussion questions

- Which two shapes did you colour blue? (1 and 6)
- What colours are shapes two and four? (both green)
- What do you notice about the colours that are on either side of the line? (they are the same)
- Can you think of anything else where the colour/pattern one side is the same as the other? (e.g. butterfly)
- Look at the shapes you coloured green. What do those numbers add up to? (6)
- If I was to change the shape that has got number 9 written on it from red to orange what other shape/number would I also have to change so that the carpet would look the same on both sides? (heart, 3)

■ Use familiar objects and common shapes to create and recreate patterns.

Date ________________

1

9

10

2

5

6

3

8

4

7

Collins New Primary Maths: Speaking and Listening Foundation © HarperCollins*Publishers* Ltd 2009

Activity 24

Foundation Understanding shape

■ Use everyday words to describe position.

Resources

Provide each child with the following:

- a copy of Activity 24 pupil sheet
- a red, blue, green, yellow and black coloured pencil or crayon

Key words

above between below behind on top of in front of over outside

Say to the children:

Listen carefully.

I am going to tell you some things to do.

I will say them only once, so listen very carefully.

Do only the things you are told to do and nothing else.

If you make a mistake, cross it out. Do not use an eraser.

There are 8 parts to this activity.

The activity

1. Look at the pot plant.
   Colour the object that is above the pot plant blue.
2. Look at the two candles.
   Colour what is between the candles green.
3. Look at the window.
   Draw a ring around the object that is below the window
4. Look at the television.
   Colour what is behind the television black.
5. Look at the small table.
   Draw a cross through the object that is on top of the coffee table.
6. Write your name on the carpet in front of the cat.
7. Look at the book.
   Colour the object that is over the book red.
8. What is outside the window?
   Colour it yellow.

Answers

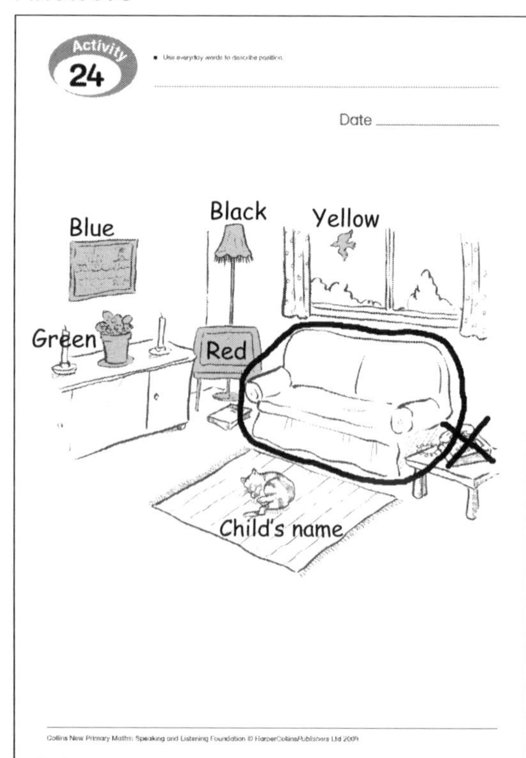

Discussion questions

↓ What is behind the television? (lamp)

↓ Which object did you colour red? (television)

■ Describe for me where the television is in this room.

■ What is in front of the window? (sofa, carpet and cat)

↑ Describe for me where the small table and the sofa are.

↑ Looking at the picture, who can describe some of the objects using the words left and right?

■ Use everyday words to describe position.

Date ________________

Activity 25

Foundation Measuring

- Use language such as 'greater' or 'smaller' to compare quantities (length).

Resources

Provide each child with the following:

- a copy of Activity 25 pupil sheet
- a coloured pencil or crayon

Key words

short/shorter/shortest long/longer/longest tall/taller/tallest
high/higher/highest thick/thicker/thickest
deep/deeper/deepest near/nearer/nearest

Say to the children:

Listen carefully.

I am going to tell you some things to do.

I will say them only once, so listen very carefully.

Do only the things you are told to do and nothing else.

If you make a mistake, cross it out. Do not use an eraser.

There are 8 parts to this activity.

The activity

1. Look at the ribbons.
   Draw a ring around the shorter ribbon.
2. Look at the birds.
   Draw a ring around the bird that is flying higher.
3. Look at the pencils.
   Draw a ring around the thickest pencil.
4. Look at the giraffes.
   Draw a ring around the taller giraffe.
5. Look at the pieces of rope.
   Draw a ring around the longest piece of rope.
6. Look at the trees.
   Write your name under the shortest tree.
7. Look at the baths.
   Draw a ring around the deepest bath.
8. Look at the children.
   Draw a ring around the child that is nearest the swing.

Answers

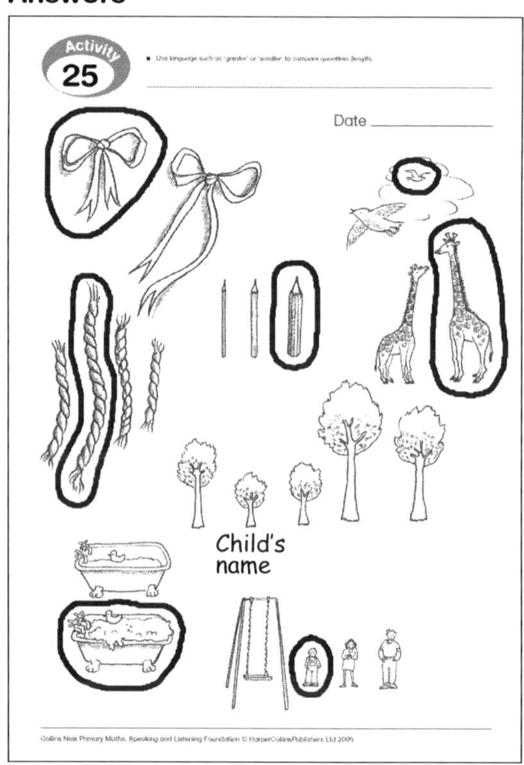

Discussion questions

- ↓ Look at the two ribbons. What can you tell me about them? How are they the same? How are they different?
- ↓ Which tree is the tallest? (4th tree)
- ■ Look at the pencils. What can you tell me about the pencil in the middle? (thicker than the 1st pencil but thinner than the 3rd pencil)
- ■ Look at the children at the bottom of the sheet. Which child is furthest from the swing? (tallest child)
- ↑ Describe the heights of the trees.
- ↑ Use the words high and low in a sentence.

■ Use language such as 'greater' or 'smaller' to compare quantities (length).

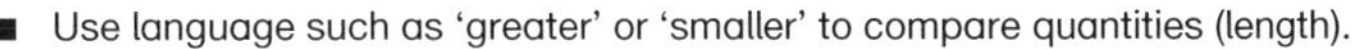

Date ____________________

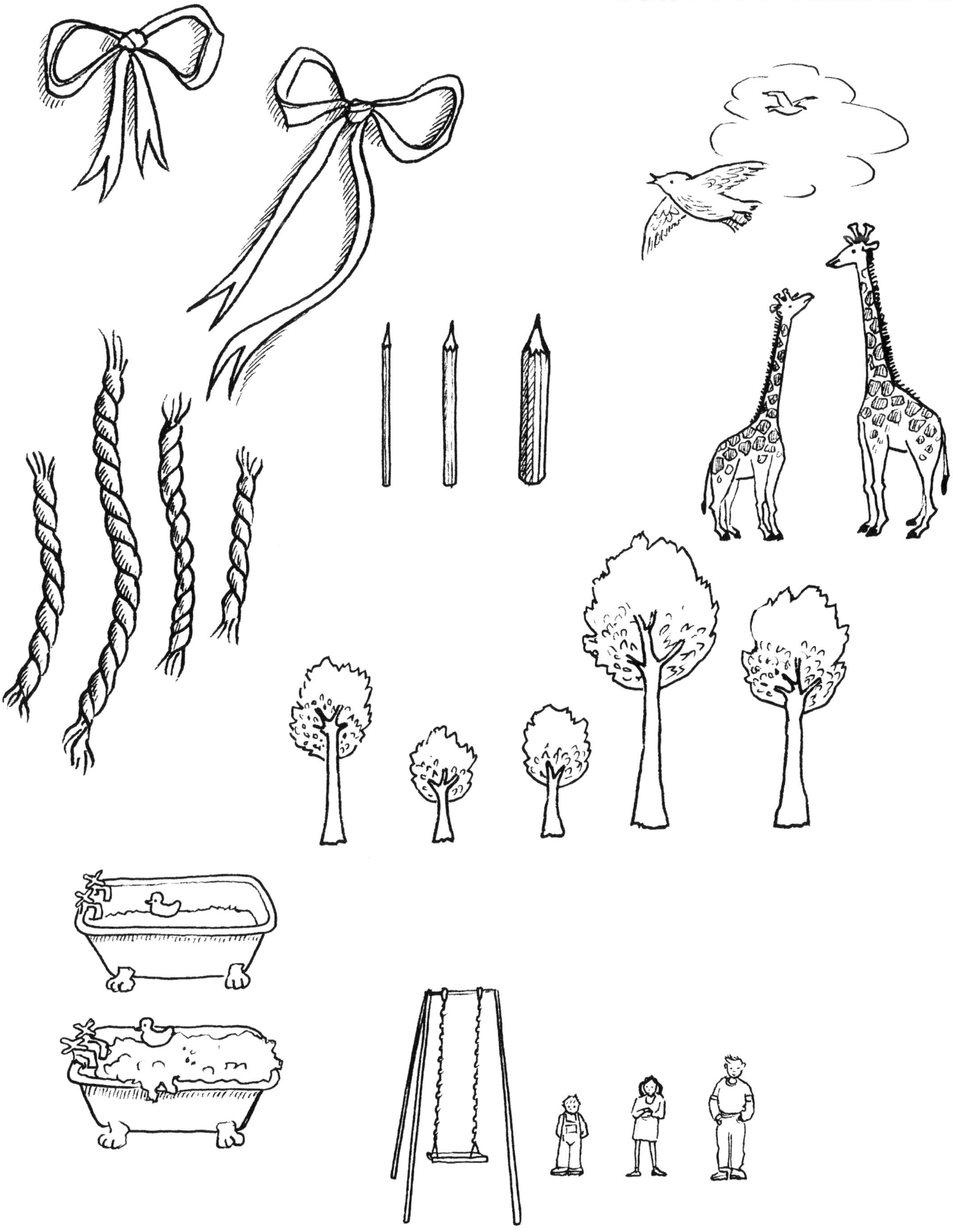

Activity 26

Foundation Measuring

- Use language such as 'greater', 'smaller', 'heavier' or 'lighter' to compare quantities (mass).

Resources

Provide each child with the following:
- a copy of Activity 26 pupil sheet
- a coloured pencil or crayon

Key words

light/lighter/lightest heavy/heavier/heaviest more

Say to the children:

Listen carefully.

I am going to tell you some things to do.

I will say them only once, so listen very carefully.

Do only the things you are told to do and nothing else.

If you make a mistake, cross it out. Do not use an eraser.

There are 7 parts to this activity.

The activity

1. Look at the man and the child.
Draw a ring around the lighter person.
2. Look at the car and the book.
Draw a ring around the heavier object.
3. Look at the kite, feather and aeroplane.
Draw a ring around the heaviest object.
4. Look at the bike, elephant, sofa, cat and pencil.
Draw a ring around the lightest object.
5. Look at the bird. In the box next to the bird draw something that is heavier than a bird.
6. Look at the truck. In the box next to the truck draw something that is lighter than a truck.
7. Look at the balance at the top of the sheet. Both these buckets have sand in them. Write your name on the bucket that has more sand in it than the other.

Answers

Discussion questions

- Which is lighter – the man or the child? (child)
- Look at the picture of the bird. What did you draw that was heavier than the bird? What else could you have drawn that was heavier than the bird? What could you have drawn that was lighter than the bird?
- Which was the heaviest: the kite, the feather or the aeroplane? (aeroplane)
- Tell me something heavier than an aeroplane. Tell me something lighter than an aeroplane.
- Of all the objects on the sheet, which do you think is the heaviest/lightest? Why?
- Look at the top of the sheet. Which bucket did you write your name on? Why?

■ Use language such as 'greater', 'smaller', 'heavier' or 'lighter' to compare quantities (mass).

Date ______________

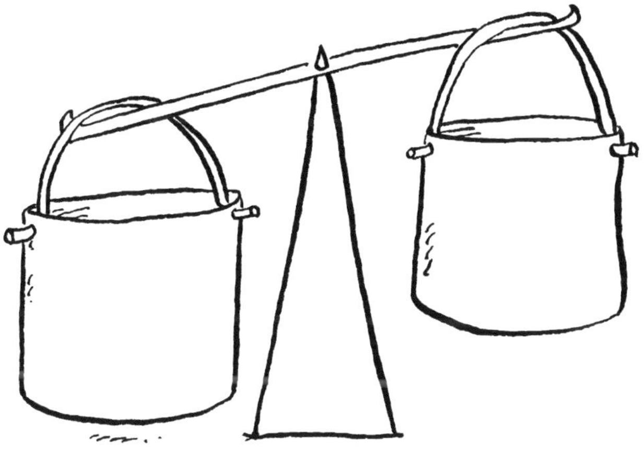

Collins New Primary Maths: Speaking and Listening Foundation © HarperCollins*Publishers* Ltd 2009

Activity 27

Foundation Measuring

- Use language such as 'greater' or 'smaller' to compare quantities (capacity).

Resources

Provide each child with the following:

- a copy of Activity 27 pupil sheet
- a coloured pencil or crayon

Key words

more most less least empty full half full

Say to the children:

Listen carefully.

I am going to tell you some things to do.

I will say them only once, so listen very carefully.

Do only the things you are told to do and nothing else.

If you make a mistake, cross it out. Do not use an eraser.

There are 8 parts to this activity.

The activity

1. Look at the buckets. Draw a ring around the bucket that can hold more water than the other.
2. Look at the baths. Draw a ring around the bath that can hold less water than the other.
3. Look at the watering can, swimming pool, sink, goldfish bowl and saucepan. Draw a ring around the object that would hold the most water.
4. Look at the cup, mug, spoon and glass. Draw a ring around the object that would hold the least water.
5. Look at the empty flowerpot. Colour the flowerpot so that it is half full with soil.
6. Look at the empty bottle of juice. Colour the bottle so that it is full with juice.
7. Look at the vase. In the box next to the vase draw something that holds more water than the vase.
8. Write your name at the top of the sheet.

Answers

Discussion questions

- ↓ Which bucket holds the most water? (large bucket)
- ↓ Look at the picture of the vase. What did you draw that holds more water than the vase? What else could you have drawn? What could you have drawn that holds less water than the vase?
- ■ Which holds the most water: the watering can, the swimming pool, the sink, the goldfish bowl or the saucepan? (swimming pool)
- ■ Tell me something that holds more water than a swimming pool. Tell me something that holds less water than a swimming pool.
- ↑ Of all the objects on the sheet which one holds the most water? Why?
- ↑ Look at the flowerpot/bottle of juice. What can you tell me about it?

■ Use language such as 'greater' or 'smaller' to compare quantities (capacity).

Date ______________

 © HarperCollins*Publishers* Ltd 2009

Activity 28

Foundation Measuring

- Use everyday language related to time; order and sequence familiar events.

Resources

Provide each child with the following:

- a copy of Activity 28 pupil sheet
- a pencil

Key words

one, two...seven first next before zebra crossing

Say to the children:

Listen carefully.

I am going to tell you some things to do.

I will say them only once, so listen very carefully.

Do only the things you are told to do and nothing else.

If you make a mistake, cross it out. Do not use an eraser.

There are 8 parts to this activity.

Answers

The activity

1. Every afternoon Simon walks home from school with his mum. Look at the school bag Simon is holding. Write your own name on Simon's bag.
2. As they walk home the first thing they pass is a post-box. Look for the picture that shows this. Write number one on the post-box.
3. The next thing Simon and his mum pass is the lamppost. Look for the picture that shows this. Write number two on the lamppost.
4. They then cross the zebra crossing. Look for the picture that shows this. Write number three on the lollipop lady's sign.
5. Simon and his mum then walk past a telephone box. Look for the picture that shows this. Write number four on the telephone box.
6. They then walk through the park. Look for the picture that shows this. Write number five on the rubbish bin.
7. Just before Simon and his mother get home they stop at the shops. Look for the picture that shows this. Write number six on one of the shop windows.
8. Simon and his mother then reach home. Look for the picture that shows this. Write number seven on Simon's front door.

Discussion questions

- ↓ What is the last thing Simon passes before reaching home? (shops)
- ↓ What number house does Simon live in? (7) How do you know?
- ■ What is the next thing Simon and his mother pass after the post-box? (lamppost)
- ■ What do Simon and his mum pass just before they walk through the park? (telephone box)
- ↑ Describe the walk Simon and his mum take from school to home every afternoon.
- ↑ Describe the walk Simon and his mum take from home to school every morning.

- Use everyday language related to time; order and sequence familiar events.

Date ____________________

Collins New Primary Maths: Speaking and Listening Foundation © HarperCollins*Publishers* Ltd 2009

Foundation Measuring

- Use everyday language related to time; order and sequence familiar events.
- (Begin to know the days of the week in order.)

Resources

Provide each child with the following:

- a copy of Activity 29 pupil sheet
- a red, blue, green and yellow coloured pencil or crayon

Key words

Monday, Tuesday…Sunday yesterday today tomorrow before after

Say to the children:

Listen carefully.

I am going to tell you some things to do.

I will say them only once, so listen very carefully.

Do only the things you are told to do and nothing else.

If you make a mistake, cross it out. Do not use an eraser.

There are 7 parts to this activity.

The activity

This activity is all about a girl called Kim. The sheet shows you some of the things Kim did last week.

1. On Tuesday Kim went to the dentist.
   Colour the word 'Tuesday' green.
2. On Sunday Kim went to visit her grandparents.
   Colour the word 'Sunday' blue.
3. Every Wednesday Kim has a piano lesson.
   Colour the word 'Wednesday' yellow.
4. What day did Kim help her dad wash the car?
   Colour that day red.
5. What day did Kim go shopping with her mother?
   Draw a ring around that day.
6. The day after Thursday Kim and her parents had a take-away meal.
   Draw a cross through that day.
7. Write your name at the top of the sheet.

Answers

Discussion questions

- ↓ You drew a ring around the word Thursday. What did Kim do on Thursday? (went shopping with her mum)
- ↓ What day did you colour yellow? (Wednesday) What does Kim do every Wednesday? (have a piano lesson)
- ■ What day is it today? What will Kim do today? What did she do yesterday? What will she do tomorrow?
- ■ What day comes before/after Thursday? (Wednesday/Friday)
- ↑ What did Kim do on Tuesday/Saturday? (went to the dentist/helped her dad wash the car)
- ↑ On what day does Kim's school have assembly? (Monday)

- Use everyday language related to time; order and sequence familiar events.
- (Begin to know the days of the week in order.)

Date ______________

Monday

Tuesday

Wednesday

Thursday

Friday

Saturday

Sunday

 © HarperCollins*Publishers* Ltd 2009

Foundation Measuring

- Use everyday language related to time.
- (Begin to read o'clock time.)

Resources

Provide each child with the following:

- a copy of Activity 30 pupil sheet
- a red, blue, green and yellow coloured pencil or crayon

Key words

clock o'clock

Say to the children:

Listen carefully.

I am going to tell you some things to do.

I will say them only once, so listen very carefully.

Do only the things you are told to do and nothing else.

If you make a mistake, cross it out. Do not use an eraser.

There are 8 parts to this activity.

The activity

1. Find the clock that says six o'clock. Colour it green.
2. Find clock c. Draw hands to make the clock read two o'clock.
3. Find the clock that says four o'clock. Colour it red.
4. Find clock g. Draw hands to make it read five o'clock.
5. Find the clock that says nine o'clock. Colour it blue.
6. Find the clock that says eleven o'clock. Colour it yellow.
7. Find clock l. Make it read eight o'clock.
8. Find the clock that says three o'clock. Write your name under the clock.

Answers

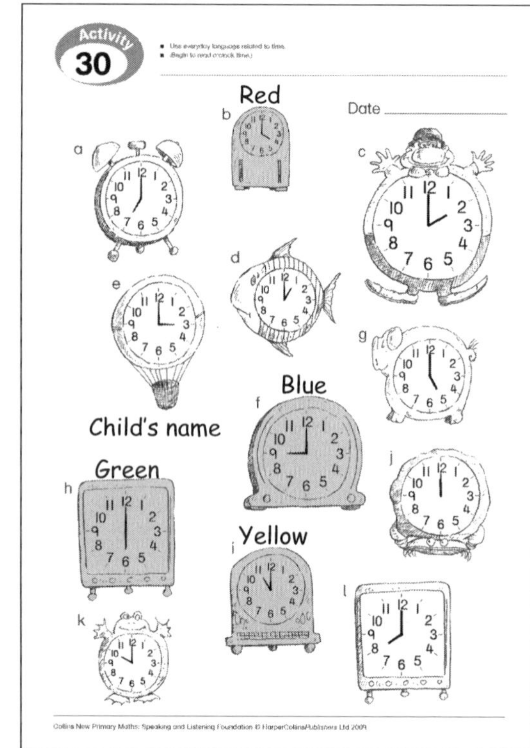

Discussion questions

- ↓ What time does clock f say? (9 o'clock)
- ↓ What time is coloured green? (6 o'clock)
- ■ Look at clock a. What time does it say? (7 o'clock)
- ■ Is there a clock that tells us the time we start/finish school? What time is that?
- ↑ Look at clock d. What time does it say? (1 o'clock) What time will it say in 2/3/5 hours' time? (3 o'clock/4 o'clock/6 o'clock)
- ↑ Look at clocks d and e. What time does clock d say? (1 o'clock) What time does clock e say? (3 o'clock) If we come in from lunch at 1 o'clock and go home at 3 o'clock, how many hours do we work after lunch before we go home? (2 hours)

- Use everyday language related to time.
- (Begin to read o'clock time.)

Date ______________

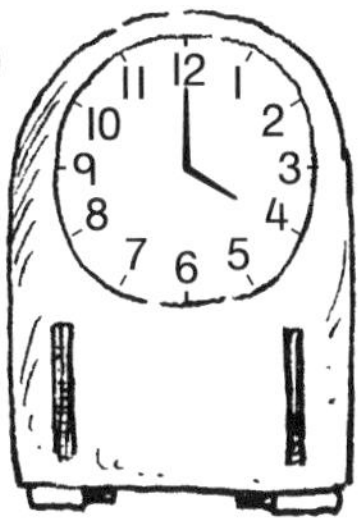

a

b

c

d

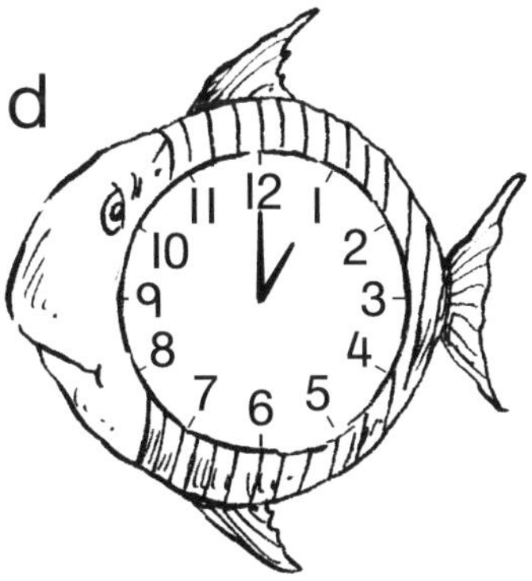

e

f

g

h

i

j

k

l